Standard Based Teaching:
A Classroom Guide

Danelle Elder

1

Library of Congress Number

ISBN-13:978-1478322580
ISBN-10:1478322586

This book is printed by Amazon.com

Contact and consulting information:
Email: daniellelelder5702@comcast.net
Website: http://standardbasedteaching.com

CONTENTS

List of Figures.. 4

List of Templates... 5

Preface.. 6

About the Author... 9

Introduction: What is Standard Based Teaching 10

Chapter 1: Creating an Accurate Target for Rubric Building 17

Chapter 2: Building a Proper Rubric 26

Chapter 3: Designing a Unit That Supports Rubric Scaffolding 38

Chapter 4: Types of Rubrics 49

Chapter 5: Organization of a Student Journal 55

Chapter 6: Student Retrieval of Scaffold Learning 61

Chapter 7: Scaffold Assessment and Reflection 68

Chapter 8: Reteach Session Using a Rubric Scaffold 76

Chapter 9: Advanced Learning 86

The Last Word.. 94

Template Appendix... 95

About The Author.. 107

LIST OF FIGURES

Figure 1   Revised Bloom's Taxonomy.. 22

Figure 2   Target Construction Example.................................... 24

Figure 3   Parts of a Rubric.. 26

Figure 4   Earth Layers Rubric.. 30

Figure 5   Writing Equations from a Scenario Rubric................ 32

Figure 6   Incorrect Rubric for No Way Out Novel................. 33

Figure 7   No Way Out Analysis Rubric.............................. 35

Figure 8   Rubric Construction Template Example................. 36

Figure 9   General Unit Planning Map.............................. 39

Figure 10   5E Learning Cycle.. 45

Figure 11   Unit Planning Guide.. 46

Figure 12   Use of the Writing Process Rubric..................... 50

Figure 13   Connecting Data Tables, Graphs and Equations Rubric...... 51

Figure 14   Volleyball Rubric.. 52

Figure 15   Target Indicators.. 53

Figure 16   Grade Indicators.. 53

Figure 17   Table of Contents.. 57

Figure 18   Journal Multitarget Assessment Rubric and Reflection........ 60

Figure 19   Surface Area Rubric.. 62

Figure 20   Study Guide for Surface Area of a Rectangular Prism........... 64

Figure 21   Effort and Achievement Reflection Rubric Example.............. 66

Figure 22   Layers of the Earth Rubric................................. 69

Figure 23   Earth Layers Assessment Example............................ 70

Figure 24   Sentence Construction Rubric............................... 71

Figure 25   Sentence Construction Assessment Example................... 72

Figure 26   Effort and Achievement Reflection Rubric Example.............. 73

Figure 27   Post Assessment and Reflection............................. 74

Figure 28   Level 1 Reteach... 79

Figure 29   Cultural Groups in Community Rubric........................ 81

Figure 30   Level 2 Cultural Groups Reteach............................ 82

Figure 31   Level 3 Cultural Groups Reteach............................ 83

Figure 32   Example of Reteach for levels 2 and 3...................... 84

Figure 33   Proficient and Advanced 4th Grade Reading Skill Characteristics   88

Figure 34   Rational Numbers Rubric................................... 90

Figure 35   Level 3 Diagramming of the Heart.......................... 91

Figure 36   Level 4 Diagramming of the Heart.......................... 91

LIST OF TEMPLATES

Target Construction Template... 96
Rubric Construction Template... 97
General Unit Map Template... 98
Unit Planning Guide Template... 100
Table of Contents... 101
Multitarget Journal Rubric Template... 102
Study Guide Template... 103
Effort and Achievement Reflection Rubric Template......................... 104
Level 1 Reteach Template.. 105
Reteach for Level 2 and 3 Template... 106

PREFACE

I have been teaching for more than 26 years.   Much of this time I spent teaching middle school science.   I spent years trying to find a system of teaching that works for all students; special education, English Second Language, regular education, emotionally-at-risk, lower socioeconomic and advanced students.

Teaching high school science and math during summers for credit retrieval has helped me stay in touch with students who have deficiencies in their learning while preparing to graduate.

Over the last several years, I developed an organizational system of teaching called Standard Based Teaching. This system is a support system for standard based grading and reporting. It is an organizational system that will help address these deficiencies and gaps in student learning while challenging advanced students.

State and district assessments have helped tighten the latitude teachers traditionally have been afforded when differentiating instruction for students who struggle with learning. Simultaneously, districts now more than ever are in a rush to find a learning fix for the students who are not graduating from high school.

Standard Based Teaching: A Classroom Guide is an organizational system that divides learning into discrete components of learning with increasing complexity. Each level is linked to the level before it.

This division in learning helps the teacher create step by step instruction that helps all students. Most importantly, it is helpful for students who find learning overwhelming. In this way, students who fail the first level know exactly where they are experiencing difficulty. The teacher then can address the deficiency or gap in learning before more complex learning is attempted by the student.

By initially identifying these learning gaps and creating an alternate learning experience for students, gaps in student learning are caught immediately. Ultimately, the student is better prepared for future subjects and grade advancement.

Everything in the Standard Based Teaching system is aligned with a standard. The targets and rubrics must be developed first from a state standard.

I have seen many inaccurate rubrics that teachers are using in their classroom. Some of these rubrics teachers have developed themselves but other poorly constructed rubrics actually are provided in curriculum materials or even in well known educational publications.

Target and rubric construction is key to clear communication about student learning. Standard Based Teaching: A Classroom Guide is a tool teachers can use to ensure targets, rubrics and all instruction are accurately aligned to a state standard.

In addition to target and rubric construction expertise, teachers need to shift their collaboration focus. Assessments should not be the focus of any team or collaboration. Instead, rubrics should be the focus, leaving the teacher the independence of assessment construction.

Districts who implement standard based grading and reporting soon find there is a missing piece. After a report card has been constructed, the actual 'standardizing' work that must go on in the classroom is not clearly defined anywhere. Teachers become frustrated and overwhelmed.

Standard Based Teaching: a Classroom Guide is an organizational system for standard based teaching will answer many of the perplexing questions teacher will have when implementing standard based grading. Teachers find the help they need when tackling standard based grading and reporting in Standard Based Teaching: A Classroom Guide.

Note: The standards used in this publication are from the Washington State Office of Public Instruction website, www.k12.wa.us. It was easier to use the standards from my home state as standard examples. However, any state standard can be substituted when using the templates in the Template Appendix.

ACKNOWLEDGEMENTS

I was a geologist before I became a teacher. Technical writing was really the only form of writing I used as a geologist. Still writing a book of this nature took every minute I could squeeze into my evenings often at the expense of my family. I would like to thank my family, Connie, Bailie, Shea and Rainey for all their patience every night while I typed.

I would like to thank my mother, Diana Elder who is an expert word-smith. She spent many evenings reading, correcting and suggesting improvements to my writing. She provided a great sense of direction for this book. For this I am ever grateful.

I would like to thank Kent Hibbard (social studies teacher) for his editing efforts.

I need to thank Diane Gibson for years spent as my cohort, collaborating and testing ideas in the classroom.

I have listened to lectures of Rick Stiggins and Ken O'Connor and found them to be inspiring. They have been 'educational warriors' fighting for change in a battlefield of educational conservatism.

I hope that Standard Based Teaching: A Classroom Guide inspires other teachers to create and publish material based on their own expertise.

INTRODUCTION:
WHAT IS STANDARD BASED TEACHING?

America's schools are under great pressure to prove that they can produce students that can pass high stakes state assessments, as well as prepare students for the ever changing work place. Districts search for professional development that will create real change in their schools. In this rush, schools have exposed teachers to a myriad of teaching concepts that will hopefully improve student learning.

Standard based grading is a system of grading which some schools and districts have implemented, that has lead to an increase in student academic performance (O'Conner, 2009).

There are two steps to standard based grading.

The step most schools focus on is **standard based reporting**, where a new report card is designed by schools and districts to report student progress on specific standards. There is now a critical mass of authors addressing standard based grading so that schools can create and launch report cards they design.

The second step of standard based grading has almost no published resources to support it, **standard based teaching**. Once a report card has been developed, determining actual classroom practice that supports standard base grading is difficult. It is important that schools not only change the way they report scores but also give teachers strategies that will prepare teachers to use standard based grading. Standard based teaching is the classroom support that teachers need to successfully implement standard based grading.

Employing the Elements of Standard Based Teaching helps create **a framework for addressing poverty, special education, second-**

language learners, advanced learners and all other students in the classroom.

What is standard based teaching? To understand this concept, it is important to first define standard based grading. Standard based grading communicates to the student a clear message of what the student has already learned and targets, based on state standards that the student has not yet mastered. Armed with the knowledge of clear targets and a grading system that reflects true learning, students are able to make informed decisions about what they should do next to master unlearned concepts. Making these informed decisions allows the student more opportunity to participate and manage their own education.

Employing the Elements of Standard Based Teaching helps create a framework for addressing poverty, special education and second-language learners.

STANDARD BASED GRADING

Standard based grading has been summed up by Tomlinson and McTighe (2006) in six principles below.

1. Grades should be based on clearly specified learning goals and performance standards. Grades are based on academically important goals. Most districts use the state developed targets for these goals.

2. Evidence used for grading should be valid. Grades should be calculated from scores that are derived only from learning the communicated goal or target. As an example, penmanship and other nontarget related factors are not used in the grade calculation.

3. Grades should be based on established criteria, not arbitrary norms. Grades are not adjusted to a bell curve. Scores are derived solely from assessments measuring content-specific criteria.

4. Not everything should be included in grades. Formative grading is not used in the final grade. Homework, for example, is not summative proof of understanding so should not be put in the grade.

5. Avoid grading based on averages (mean). A score derived from averaging only informs students about how much they did not learn. Scores should inform students and teachers alike, as to which concepts have been mastered and which have not.

6. Factors such as effort, participation, attendance, homework, etc. should be addressed separately. Factors that are not directly related to the academic target should not be included in a score like participation, attendance, and attitude. While important to the student's education, those factors should be reported separately so that scores clearly show only a reflection of target mastery.

Schools now can concentrate on clearly informing students of the concepts that must be mastered.

Using the above Principles of Standard Based Grading (Tomlinson and McTighe, 2006), schools are changing the way they communicate with students. Schools now can concentrate on clearly informing students of the concepts that must be mastered. For districts who have implemented standard based grading, these concepts or targets are the main focus of the teacher throughout the school year.

Educational experts like Guskey, O'Conner, Stiggins and others have helped convince many school districts that it is time to end decades of grading by the mean system.

In the mean system of grading, when a student receives a score of 59%, this score is typically interpreted as a failure or an F. This type of report of student progress about learning does not tell a student what they have not mastered. It does not give the student credit for any learning even though the student learned more than half of the material. More importantly, the message sent to the student is a message of failure.

In standard based grading system, learning is approached incrementally. Students are given grades by level of understanding, the level of scaffold understanding they have learned (O'Conner 2007).

Asking teachers to abandon a well understood practice like the mean grading system and substitute standard based grading, needs the implementation of a well thought out system of classroom strategies to help guide teachers.

This publication will provide a concrete and highly useful method of teaching and communicating with students that is necessary to implement standard based grading.

ELEMENTS OF STANDARD BASED TEACHING:

There are nine elements to standard based teaching.

1. <u>Creating an accurate target for rubric building</u>
State standards are often constructed with multiple attributes or in language the student cannot understand. It is imperative that the target be properly constructed for clear communication about learning.

2. <u>Building a proper rubric</u>
Rubrics must be built in levels where logical steps scaffold learning from foundational learning, bridging knowledge and finally target mastery.

3. <u>Designing a unit that supports rubric scaffolding</u>
Units need to be designed to teach at each level in the rubric. Using a unit template that is set up for rubric support makes this task far easier for the teacher.

4. <u>Types of rubrics</u>
Rubrics can be created for different purposes. The most common type is the Single Concept Rubric. Rubrics can also be designed for processes or procedures.

5. Organization of a Student Journal

Student journaling is the most effective and organized method of tracking formative assessment of student understanding. Journals are organized in rubric levels and color coded accordingly.

6. Student Retrieval of Scaffold Learning and Reflection

Study guides must tell the student what to review, how to review and be diagnostic as to whether or not the student has learned targets. Study guide scaffolding also matches all previous scaffolding, set up by the rubric. After students complete the study guide, students fill out a reflection about what they have learned and the effort they have put into learning.

7. Scaffold assessment

Like everything taught before it, the learning should be assessed by the levels in the rubric: foundational (level 1), bridge to target (level 2); and target mastery (level 3).

8. Reteach session using a rubric scaffold

If students are not successful in passing the summative assessment, they are given another chance to master targets, starting with the level the student did not master.

Teachers are being asked to construct targets and rubrics without proper training.

9. Advanced learning

Some students will need a learning challenge that goes beyond target mastery. This is advanced learning or level 4. This can be done in project form, such as an extra advanced assignment per quarter or as part of regular assessments.

It is clear from examining the Elements of Standard Based Teaching that targets and rubrics are central. Currently, teachers are being asked to construct targets and rubrics without proper training. This often results in errors that create confusion about learning for both students and teachers. Rubrics must be scaffolded or chucked properly, dividing the target into understandable, learnable and logical steps for student mastery. Without well constructed rubrics, teachers are no better off using standard based grading than when they used the mean system to produce a grade. Students must be given step by step information about where they are in the process of mastering each target.

Since standards vary from state to state, publishers of curricula cannot be expected to create targets for classroom use. Once teachers are taught how to make a proper target and rubric, they will be able to develop targets and rubrics for any subject or content. *Standard Based Teaching: A Classroom Guide* is designed to provide examples and templates for teachers to use so they may successfully implement standard based grading.

Two types of learning goals will be considered in this publication: **product and progress goals**. Guskey (2010) defines product goals as 'what students should know and be able to do at a certain point in time'. Progress goals are defined as goals that measure how much improvement the student has made toward a goal or target. Rubric construction for both product and process goals is similar. Guskey uses 'goal' when describing a proficiency outcome. For *Standard Based Teaching: A Classroom Guide*, the term, 'target' will be interchanged for the word 'goal'.

Once mastering target and rubric construction, **teachers must move from thinking of themselves as facilitators of a particular content to researchers of learning.**

It is becoming the job of the teacher to collect and examine data about student learning progression in target mastery. This data collection is a new domain for most teachers. Data must be collected and analyzed in real time. After examining students scores, the teacher can then, determine whether the student is ready to move up to a different learning level on the rubric ultimately progressing toward mastering the target. **Therefore, teachers must be come a classroom analyst of the student scores.**

The Elements to Standard Based Teaching were developed in this way: data kept over time on student learning pitted against the constant backdrop of teacher practices. Ultimately, a new system of teaching was created that was grounded in student data and supported by an increase in learning by students.

In this publication, there are student and teacher templates to help simplify transitioning from the mean system of grading to standard based grading. A few of these templates are only meant to be used as a trainer. Other templates are designed for regular use by teachers. Teachers may want to alter the templates as they become proficient at standard based teaching.

All the targets in Standard Based Teaching: A Classroom Guide were constructed from Washington State standards. Any state standards, however, can be used with the templates. **The following chapters will provide information necessary to begin to develop a profile of students as a learner.**

References:

Guskey, Thomas R., Bailey, Jane M., (2010). *Developing Standards-Based Report Cards.* Thousand Oaks, CA: Corwin

O Conner, K. (2009). How to Grade for Learning K-12 (3rd Ed.), Corwin, Thousand Oaks, CA

O'Conner, K. (2007). *A Repair Kit for Grading: 15 Fixes for Broken Grades*, ETS/ATI. Portland, OR

Payne, R. K. (1998/2005). *A Framework for Understanding Poverty* (4th Ed.). Highlands, TX:RFT Publishing.

Stiggins, Richard J. (2006). *Assessment for Learning: A key to Motivation and Achievement.* Edge

Tomlinson, C. A., & McTighe, J. (2006). *Integrating Differentiated Instruction and Understanding by Design.* Alexandria, VA: ASCD

CHAPTER 1:
CREATING AN ACCURATE TARGET FOR RUBRIC BUILDING

Standard based teaching requires teachers to become fluent in target interpretation and construction.

A properly constructed rubric is the heart of standard based grading. Without a well constructed rubric, implementing standard based grading is impossible. The core of any rubric is the target. Targets used for rubric construction usually must be developed from the list of state targets. Constructing a target to teach is not as simple as copying a standard from a state website and using it in the classroom. **There are important guidelines that must be observed in writing an accurate target.** Therefore, when implementing standard based grading teachers need to become fluent at target interpretation and construction.

Standard Component:
A portion of a state standard that has a single attribute.

To construct an accurate target, it is important to consider these guidelines:

- Targets should be written to **empower students** to ask themselves about target mastery
- Targets must be written in **student friendly language**
- Targets should be constructed with only **one standard component from the state standard**
- Targets must be assessed on language that is associated with a state standard , not language that depicts behavior
- Targets should be assessed on the **level of complexity given in the state standard**
- Targets should **reflect important content** inside each subject area

Target:
A standard component that is written in student friendly language and is level 3 or proficient learning in a rubric.

TARGET EXAMPLES AND CONSTRUCTION

<u>Targets should be written to empower students to ask themselves about target mastery.</u> Students should positively express what they have learned. To do this they must answer the question, "Can I show evidence that I understand this target?" Targets should be written in '**I can**' form, as in the example below.

I can use elaborations to develop my ideas in the writing process.

From reading the target, there is only one question that a student needs to answer, "Can I or can't I use elaborations to develop my ideas?" Well-written targets and rubrics boil information down to this simple decision: a **yes** or **no** question about learning.

> It is the student who must regularly use a rubric to assess their own level of learning readiness.

<u>Targets must be written in student friendly language.</u> It is the student who must regularly use a rubric to assess their own level of learning readiness. It would be counterproductive then if the rubrics were written in language the student could not understand. For example, the following target was taken from a state standard and not modified except to add an **I can** to the beginning.

I can use multiple pre-reading strategies in a variety of genres to help me understand what I have read.

The language difficulty for this target is too high. This target is too complicated for the student to answer the ever important question, "Can I or can't I show evidence I understand this target?" However, the target language must be simplified without compromising the meaning of the state standard.

I can use different pre-reading strategies to understand several styles of writing.

<u>Targets should be constructed with only one attribute from the state standard.</u> Having more than one standard component or facet to a rubric completely defeats the point of constructing a rubric. Using multiple concepts for a single rubric creates

confusion and leads to failure to master the target. Only a single standard component can be expressed and subsequently assessed. When state standard incorporate several component they must be separated into individual targets.

I can read and create a scatterplot to solve a problem.

This target has two attributes. **Reading** a scatterplot and **creating** a scatterplot are distinctly different standard components. The filter for separating the two standard components is asking the question:"Are reading and creating scatterplots taught with different skills or content? " If they are different then two different strategies for the teaching are needed to master two entirely different standard components. They then cannot be put in the same target unless the target is the culmination of a learning process where several targets have been used over time to evaluate a learning progression. Progress rubrics will be discussed in Chapter 4: Types of Rubrics.

Once separated into two targets, they should read:

I can read a scatterplot to solve a problem.

I can create a scatterplot to solve a problem.

Now each target can be put into a separate rubric or in different levels of a process rubric.

<u>Targets must be assessed on language that is associated with state standards but language that depicts behavior.</u>

The evaluation of a students writing must adhere to the language specified by the state target.

I can use writing conventions accurately done in ink.

The important points of the target above are that the student be able to demonstrate *accurate use of writing conventions*. Unless a state target requires the use of **ink**, the student cannot be evaluated for the use of ink in their writing. Ink is a **condition of writing**.

If a teacher wants students writing to be in ink then the teacher should not accept the writing in anything but ink. The student should be given back the work in pencil and told that the writing is not ready to be evaluated. The student should be informed that once the writing is done in ink, it will be scored.

Another example of improper target language can be seen in the following:

I can use symbols accurately and neatly in my writing.

In the above target, unless neatness is specified in the state target, it cannot be inserted into the rubric. Assessing whether a student can use symbols accurately does not rely on neatness. Neatness is not an academic attribute but a condition of writing. If a teacher wants student work to be neat, then the work should not be accepted until the work is in that condition. Neatness has mastered how to use symbols correctly. The target should read:

I can use symbols accurately in my writing.

<u>Targets should be assessed for their level of complexity (level of Bloom's).</u>

When constructing a target from a state standard, the complexity of the standard must be first assessed. There is a difference between difficulty and complexity of a task or target (Sousa 2001). Teachers often increase the level of difficulty without increasing the complexity of the task or target. To determine the level of complexity, compare the state standard language to (figure 1) Bloom's Taxonomy of learning (revised Anderson 1990). It is important that the language in the target has the same complexity as the state standard.

I can use at least six elaborations to develop my ideas.

The above target adds difficulty without adding complexity of learning. The student should only be required to show evidence that they can use elaborations in developing an ideas or set of ideas. Assessing if a student can use 6 versus 3 elaborations only adds difficulty not complexity. Using 3 elaborations can show mastery of elaboration development. Determining a target must be dependant on the student completing the proper complexity level, not the proper number of examples.

Some words used in targets are too general and do not communicate a concept clearly.

I can understand the components of health-related fitness.

In this target, the word "understand" can evoke a variety of interpretations for both the teacher to assess and the student. Using the Bloom's Taxonomy list of key words can aid in creating a much more accurate target. Some possible terms that could be used to substituted for **understand** are *apply, demonstrate, state and many others.*

I can apply the components of health related fitness to a sport.

This target is much clearer as to what the student will understand what to do to show mastery.

<u>Targets should reflect important content inside each subject area</u>

Many districts have begun to prioritize learning standards. They have recognized that some standards are more important than others, power standards (Henderson 2009). Other standards are sub-standards or supportive standards. Supporting standards may still need to be reviewed or taught but assessments should determine mastery of the most important standards.

The student will experience and analyze a variety of art styles and genres.

In the standard, experiencing the art styles may be difficult to assess. The student can be exposed to a variety of art styles and genres but only assessed on the student's ability to analyze them.

Revised Bloom's Taxonomy:
A changed Bloom's taxonomy that combines analysis and synthesis and adds creativity as the highest level.

Figure 1

Revised Bloom's Taxonomy

Category	Example and Key Words (verbs)
Remembering: Recall previous learned information.	**Examples**: Recite a policy. Quote prices from memory to a customer. Knows the safety rules. **Key Words**: defines, describes, identifies, knows, labels, lists, matches, names, outlines, recalls, recognizes, reproduces, selects, states.
Understanding: Comprehending the meaning, translation, interpolation, and interpretation of instructions and problems. State a problem in one's own words.	**Examples**: Rewrites the principles of test writing. Explain in one's own words the steps for performing a complex task. Translates an equation into a computer spreadsheet. **Key Words**: comprehends, converts, defends, distinguishes, estimates, explains, extends, generalizes, gives an example, infers, interprets, paraphrases, predicts, rewrites, summarizes, translates.
Applying: Use a concept in a new situation or unprompted use of an abstraction. Applies what was learned in the classroom into novel situations in the work place.	**Examples**: Use a manual to calculate an employee's vacation time. Apply laws of statistics to evaluate the reliability of a written test. **Key Words**: applies, changes, computes, constructs, demonstrates, discovers, manipulates, modifies, operates, predicts, prepares, produces, relates, shows, solves, uses.
Analyzing: Separates material or concepts into component parts so that its organizational structure may be understood. Distinguishes between facts and inferences.	**Examples**: Troubleshoot a piece of equipment by using logical deduction. Recognize logical fallacies in reasoning. Gathers information from a department and selects the required tasks for training. **Key Words**: analyzes, breaks down, compares, contrasts, diagrams, deconstructs, differentiates, discriminates, distinguishes, identifies, illustrates, infers, outlines, relates, selects, separates.
	Examples: Select the most effective solution. Hire the most

Evaluating: Make judgments about the value of ideas or materials.	qualified candidate. Explain and justify a new budget. **Key Words**: appraises, compares, concludes, contrasts, criticizes, critiques, defends, describes, discriminates, evaluates, explains, interprets, justifies, relates, summarizes, supports.
Creating: Builds a structure or pattern from diverse elements. Put parts together to form a whole, with emphasis on creating a new meaning or structure.	**Examples**: Write a company operations or process manual. Design a machine to perform a specific task. Integrates training from several sources to solve a problem. Revises and process to improve the outcome. **Key Words**: categorizes, combines, compiles, composes, creates, devises, designs, explains, generates, modifies, organizes, plans, rearranges, reconstructs, relates, reorganizes, revises, rewrites, summarizes, tells, writes

TARGET CONSTRUCTION TEMPLATE

The Target Construction Template is an introductory activity for administrators and teachers for accurate target construction. Once target construction becomes routine, teachers probably will not need to use the Target Construction Template. However, some teachers may already be constructing targets inaccurately so it is a good idea to have even the experienced teacher use the template as well.

Users simply fill in the blanks and go through the check off list. Using the target construction guidelines, target construction is easy to master.

Figure 2 is an example of the Target Construction Template. This template is located in the Template Appendix.

Figure 2

Target Construction Example

State Standard:
Represent addition and subtraction of fractions and mixed numbers using visual and numerical models, and connect the representation to the related equation.

If the state standard has more than one attribute list each below with the supporting content.
- *Addition of fractions using visuals or numerical models*
- *Subtraction of fractions using visual or numerical models*
- *Addition of mixed numbers using visuals or numerical models*
- *Subtraction of mixed numbers using visuals or numerical models*
- *Connect with representation to the related equation*

Select one of the above attributes for target construction.

Determine the complexity according to Bloom's. List complexity level below.
Complexity Level: *application- addition of fractions*
Alternate words that can be used for attribute verb: *none*

I can: *add fractions* using *number lines, pictures and manipulatives*
      (action attribute verb)   *(use student friendly language for content)*

Target Check List

Make sure your target has:
- No numbers
- Single sentence
- A single verb
- Age appropriate vocabulary
- Important to the content
- No language that is outside of target content *(i.e. complete in ink, neatness)*

Other learning associated with this standard:

I can subtract fractions using number lines, pictures and manipulatives
I can add mixed numbers using number lines, pictures and manipulatives
I can subtract mixed numbers using number lines, pictures and manipulatives

It is important to note, in the target construction example above, the process of adding and subtracting fractions and mixed numbers are a similar process. Sousa (2001) states that, "Two concepts that are very similar to each other should not be taught at the same time" because the learner can not discern the 'critical attributes' that distinguish one from another. The concepts are overlapped in the learning process so the student has difficulty distinguishing them apart.

References:

Anderson, L.W. & Krathwohl, D.R. (Eds.) (2001). *Taxonomy for Learning, Teaching, and Assessing: A Revision of Bloom's Taxonomy of Educational Objectives.* New York: Addison Wesley Longman.

Bloom, B.S. (Ed.), Engelhart, M.D., Furst, E.J., Hill, W.H., & Krathwohl, D.R. (1956). *Taxonomy of Educational Objectives: Handbook I: Cognitive Domain.* New York: David McKay.

Henderson, Aaron, (2009). *Power Standards In Education,* www.slideshare.net/aaronhenderson/power-standards-in-education

Office of Superintendent of Public Instruction, www.k12.wa.us

Sousa, D. A. (2nd Ed). (2001) *How the Brain Learns.* Crowin Press, Thousand Oaks, California

CHAPTER 2:
BUILDING A PROPER RUBRIC

Accurate target construction is the foundation of standard based teaching and reporting. The rubric then is the framework for standard based teaching. It is essential that the rubric is constructed properly. A standard based grade that is derived from an improperly constructed rubric adds no more clarity to learning than using the mean system of grading. Poorly constructed rubrics mislead students about primary target information and the learning progression. Rubrics must be constructed consistently and in a scaffold manner. **Teachers should be collaborating on rubric construction, not assessment construction.**

A properly constructed rubric answers important questions like:

➤ How do students attack this learning target?
➤ What is the progression of learning to reach the target mastery?
➤ What is the proficient level of learning students need to do to master the target?
➤ What do students need to study for the assessment?
➤ How do students link foundational learning with the more complex target learning?

Figure 3

Indicators of a Rubric

Incomplete Evidence of Learning (I)	Level 1: Foundation for Target	Level 2: Progressing Toward Target Proficiency	Level 3: Target Proficiency	Level 4: Advanced Application of Target

THE FOUR INDICATORS OF A RUBRIC

A properly scaffold rubric has four parts. Each level advances in complexity (Figure 3). Each level builds on the learning until a deep and complete understanding of the target has been developed.

Level 1: The Foundation

Foundation: (Level 1) The most basic information needed to understand a target...usually this level is vocabulary.

If the target has sufficient vocabulary wrapped up in its understanding then that vocabulary is foundational (level 1) to understanding the target at a proficient level. If foundational material is not clearly defined and taught before the more complex target is taught, students will perform poorly on target assessments and believe they are not able to comprehend the target.

If vocabulary is not the focus of the foundational level then the teacher must assess what is the proper underlying understanding for that target that is critical for target learning. Payne (2003) reports that students living in lower socio-economic conditions are likely to have limited vocabulary. By the time student's graduate, they are potentially missing thousands of words that middle- and upper-socio economic students have acquired. This deficit is part of the reason students do not perform well on state assessments. Vocabulary then is the place to begin a unit.

It is best to start a unit with an engaging introductory activity. After this introductory activity, foundational or level 1 activities should follow. Level 1 is the lowest Bloom's Taxonomy level in the rubric: recall or recognition. An assessment can be given after level 1 has been taught to determine if this foundational knowledge has been mastered. Students should not go to level 2, until the foundation is set.

Level 2: The Bridge

After the foundational level has been constructed for a target, the next content determined is a bridging concept (Sousa 2001) linking the foundational knowledge to the target. Level 2, the bridge, is only a portion of the target. It may incorporate some or all the foundational vocabulary.

Bridge:
(Level 2) A simple concept that links target vocabulary to the target.

Target Proficiency:
(Level 3) A state standard component that is worded in student friendly language.

For example, a target may require students to evaluate the relationship of a target component (upper level Bloom's). Students may be asked to create a comparison about that component. Defining all the components might be the foundation of the target (Remembering, lowest level of Blooms Taxonomy revised 2001). The bridge for that target must be an action that is in between the two levels and link the foundation to the target action. The student may be required to explain the order of components in a diagram. This is Understanding level in Bloom's revised.

The time spent learning each level is not necessarily 33% of the time allotted for the unit. For level 2, the time should be gauged by how well students are beginning to apply the foundation knowledge to a simplified aspect of the target. This level does not require mastery of the complete target, so only formative assessments should be used.

Level 3: Target Proficiency

Level 3 is the target. After a student completes all levels of learning, the student should have a proficient understanding of the target. The level of complexity is usually upper level Bloom's Taxonomy. If the state standard is written at a middle level complexity, then the target is then middle level too.

Level 4: Advanced Understanding

Advanced Understanding: (level 4) Learning that is more complex and goes beyond target learning.

This level is advanced learning requires students to learn more than the target learning. Students should not get level 4 credit for handing in neat work or work that is always complete or thorough. Neither of these examples is learning at the advanced level. The student needs to master a much more complex concept that uses the target in an advanced way. Content beyond the target may be added. This level is covered in more detail in Chapter 9.

RUBRIC USE AND CONSTRUCTION

Rubric construction, like target construction, takes practice.

When a rubric is used to build a unit, the teacher scrutinizes each activity and assessment through the filter of the rubric. No assignment or assessments are given that are not aligned with the rubric. Students, then clearly understand what they have mastered, what has not been mastered and what to do next to provide evidence of learning.

Rubric construction, like target construction, takes practice. It is helpful to have curriculum handy when constructing a rubric. Sometimes the curricular reading already has some rubric ideas that can be used, to construct a rubric.

Departments and school staff should collaborate with previously established targets and rubrics, checking each others work for correct formatting. Departments and schools should agree that the targets and rubrics that are designed are correct.

EXAMPLES OF PROPER RUBRIC CONSTRUCTION

The following are examples of two properly constructed rubrics that are scaffolded around a well constructed target (figure 4 and 5). Notice the language at the top of each level says **target** and not **standard**. The teacher needs to create the targets because state standards are not properly written as a target. The audience and the purpose for state standards are different than the purpose of a target used in the classroom. State standards provide the scope and sequence for the development of all subjects. They are often large complex ideas that communicate information about standards to administrators, teachers, parents, colleges, and sometimes students. Targets and standards then, are not interchangeable.

A target is a single, easy to understand idea expressly designed to communicate learning in the classroom.
State Standard: Sketch and label the major layers of the Earth showing properties of each layer.

Figure 4

Earth Layers Rubric

Incomplete Evidence of Learning (I)	Level 1: Foundation for Target	Level 2: Progressing Toward Target Proficiency	Level 3: Target Proficiency	Level 4: Advanced Application of Target
	I can define: Crust Mantle Core : Inner Outer Lithosphere Asthenosphere Oceanic Crust Continental Crust	I can properly **diagram** the layers of the Earth.	I can **describe** the properties of each layer of the Earth including: Thickness Consistency Temperature Composition	I can determine the different Earth layers by **analyzing** sound wave data.

In the Earth Layers Rubric (Figure 4), the level 1 foundational learning is the vocabulary that the student will need to be successful at understanding the target. The vocabulary list should not be more than seven or eight words long. More than that will create unnecessary difficultly and distract from the important target-related words students should focus on. The teacher will have to select only the words that are absolutely necessary to understand the target.

For level 2, students are required to draw and label the layers of the Earth. This requires knowledge of thickness and the name for each layer. This is a very low level application of the target but one that can bridge the more complex target to the foundational vocabulary.

The complete target, level 3, requires students to learn layer properties. A student should be able to be given a description of a layer's temperature, for example and determine which layer is represented and other associated properties.

It is important to note that the state standard for level 3 does not require upper level Bloom's Taxonomy. The standard only requires the student to draw, label and describe the layers of the Earth. No higher level of Bloom's Taxonomy is needed to meet the standard.

Many teachers have difficulty understanding what to do with level 4. Often teachers make this level more difficult without adding complexity. This level is advanced understanding of the target and should not be included in the proficiency level of learning.

Many teachers
have difficulty
understanding
what to do with
level 4.

State Standard: Write an equation that corresponds to a given problem situation

Figure 5

Writing Equations from a Scenario Rubric

Incomplete Evidence Of Learning (I)	Level 1 Foundation for Target	Level 2 Progressing Toward Target Proficiency	Level 3 Target Proficiency	Level 4 Advanced Application of Target
	I can read a scenario and construct a data table from the scenario information.	I can construct a corresponding graph from the data table.	I can construct a corresponding equation from a graph.	I can describe the relationship of two graphs by comparing their equations.

Level 4 is for advanced mastery (Figure 5) and is more complex than the target.

Level 4 goes beyond target proficiency so is a higher level of Bloom's and so is more complex. In this case the teacher adds some new content, sound waves, to create an advanced learning opportunity.

EXAMPLES OF INCORRECT RUBRICS

Because rubric construction takes practice, it is likely that errors will be made when first attempting to create a correct rubric. The following rubric (Figure 6) has incorrect components. Seeing these mistakes may help teachers to avoid making them in the future.

State Standard: Demonstrate understanding of an author's use of literary elements and literary devices.

Figure 6

Incorrect Rubric for *No Way Out* Novel

Struggling	Emerging	Proficient	Exemplary
A *few* symbols are neatly drawn in color. Five or fewer symbols are shown. Symbols are basic.	*Some* symbols are neatly drawn in color. A minimum of 6 symbols are shown. Choice of symbols is basic and concrete.	*Most* symbols are neatly drawn in color. A minimum of 8 symbols are shown. Choice of symbols shows *some* higher level, creative thinking.	*All* symbols are neatly drawn in color. A minimum of 8 symbols are shown. Choice of symbols shows higher level, creative thinking.

Looking at the rubric level titles, level 1 states that the student is struggling. Telling a student that they are struggling does little to inform them about what they have learned and what they have not mastered.

Also, this rubric was handed out to students in a language arts class with no title. It was designed to analyze events and symbols that occurred in a novel called *No Way Out* (Hayes 2011). Rubrics always need titles. Students should have a copy of the rubric placed in their journal or a notebook for each class. The point of a rubric is a tool to increase student understanding and should be as useful and easy to understand as possible. If the student has several rubrics (all or some with no title) then the likelihood of student is confusion is increased.

In Figure 6, the teacher has substituted the word **symbols** for **literary elements and literary devices**. Literary elements are character, plot, and genre. Literary devices are simile, metaphor, personification alliteration. The target has been over simplified by substituting the word 'symbol' for the list of literary elements or devices. It is important to keep the target as similar to state standard language as possible to reduce this type of inaccuracy.

Neatness is also a requirement in this rubric. Neatness cannot be an academic goal unless a state standard requires neatness. If a teacher wants an assignment to be neat then the teacher should not accept the student's work until it is turned in neatly written. <u>Neatness is a condition of an assignment not a learning attribute.</u>

Coloring is also not a proper attribute of a learning target unless the state standard requires color. Color is not an academic goal but an assignment condition. Color cannot be scored.

The word **most** is too vague in the target. The student has to have some innate understanding of **most**. **Most** could mean any score above 50%.

When a target is written appropriately, the question of student proficiency is a **yes** or **no** choice. Guskey (2010) calls this method of pass or fail grade determination, a **dichotomous decision**. The student either shows enough evidence that they have mastered the target or not. Looking at level 1 and 2, only one thing can be determined from this rubric, that mastery of the target has not been achieved. There is no foundational building or bridging between level 1 and 3. The student is given no information as to where to begin learning the target or how to proceed once level 1 has been achieved.

Also in this rubric, there is no real difference between the level of learning between level 3 and level 4. A perfect score does not show advanced thinking about the target.

In the corrected rubric below (figure 7), the levels now are properly scaffolded.

Neatness is not an academic standard.

Dichotomous decision: A decision that is answered as either 'I know it' or 'I don't know it'. There is nothing in between.

Figure 7

State Standard: Demonstrate understanding of an author's use of literary elements and literary devices.

No Way Out Analysis Rubrics

Incomplete Evidence Of Learning (I)	Level 1 Foundational Learning for Standard	Level 2 Progressing Toward Standard	Level 3 Meeting Standard	Level 4 Advanced Application of Standard
	I can define: Literary elements: • Setting • Mood • Character • Plot Literary devices: • Metaphor • Simile • Alliteration • Personification	I can give an example an of a literary element/ device from the novel <u>No Way Out</u>	I can show how a literary element/ device relates to the novel <u>No Way Out</u>	I can compare literary elements/ devices from <u>No Way Out</u> to another novel.

Below is a Rubric Construction Example (figure 8). This template can be found in the Appendix for Templates. Using this template, all the standard information is preserved. Occasionally the same standard will have more than one target associated with it. It is worth making sure the complete standard is written with each rubric so other related targets taught later can be sequenced properly.

Figure 8

Rubric Construction Example

Topic: Math
Unit: *Graphing whole numbers/rational numbers*
State Standard Classification: *8.4.D*
State Standard: *Identify rational and irrational numbers.*
Target: *The student will graph positive and negative whole numbers*
Rubric Title: *Rational Numbers*

Incomplete Evidence of Learning (I)	Level 1: Foundation for Target	Level 2: Progressing Toward Target Proficiency	Level 3: Target Proficiency	Level 4: Advanced Application of Target
No evidence of meeting standard	*I can...* *define/diagram:* *Negative* *Positive* *Plot* *Whole numbers* *Decimal numbers*	*I can...* *plot both negative and positive whole numbers*	*I can...* *graph both negative and positive whole numbers*	*I can...* *graph both negative and positive decimal numbers*

References:

Anderson, L.W. & Krathwohl, D.R. (Eds.) (2001*). Taxonomy for Learning, Teaching, and Assessing: A Revision of Bloom's Taxonomy of Educational Objectives.* New York: Addison Wesley Longman.

Bloom, B.S. (Ed.), Engelhart, M.D., Furst, E.J., Hill, W.H., & Krathwohl, D.R. (1956). *Taxonomy of Educational Objectives: Handbook I: Cognitive Domain.* New York: David McKay. Guskey, Thomas R., Bailey, Jane M., (2010). *Developing Standards-Based Report Cards.* Thousand Oaks, CA: Corwin

Hayes, Kathie, and Ed Hayes. *No Way Out.* 1st ed. Seattle, WA: Books To Go Now, 2011. Digital

Office of Superintendent of Public Instruction, www.k12.wa.us

CHAPTER 3:
DESIGNING A UNIT THAT SUPPORTS RUBRIC SCAFFOLDING

General Unit Map:
A planning guide that has important unit information. It is not tightly scripted so teachers that collaborate have curricular structure with some individual flexibility.

All assignments and assessments for each unit must be aligned to a properly constructed rubric. Two tools can be used to create a unit plan, the General Unit Map and Unit Planning Guide.

GENERAL UNIT MAP TEMPLATE

A General Unit Map (Figure 9) can be used to help teachers set up a unit where key information, assignments and assessments are aligned with a specific rubric. This is helpful if teachers collaborate and team members want to solidify key elements of a unit plan but leave room for individualization.

In the example below, all important teaching information is included in the unit map so that teachers can file the plan away when done with the unit, ready for the next year.

Unit Planning Guide:
A guide that has all information about a specific unit.

The template for the unit plan is in the Template Appendix.

The top section of the General Unit Map contains the content area, standard, target and rubric.

Figure 9

General Unit Map Example

General Unit Map				
Content Area: *Earth Science*				
State Standard: *Draw a labeled diagram showing how convection in the upper mantle drives movement of crustal plates*				
Learning Target (s): *Students will be able to diagram events that occur at the plate boundaries including the boundaries of the Pacific Northwest* **Rubric Title:** *Plate Tectonics*				
Incomplete Evidence of Learning (I)	**Level 1** Foundational for Target	**Level 2** Progressing Toward Target Proficiency	**Level 3** Target Proficiency	**Level 4** Advanced Application of Target
	(lower level Bloom's) I can … <ul><li>draw/define</li><li>crustal plates</li><li>crust</li><li>mantle</li><li>core</li><li>convection current</li></ul>	(middle level Bloom's) I can… *diagram the convection currents that drive crustal plates*	(upper level Bloom's) I can… *diagram events that occur at the plate boundaries including the boundaries of the Pacific Northwest*	(high Bloom's) I can… *predict how future movement of plates will change the shape/location of continents*

	Unit Detail Section	
Date Days	**Elicitation Question:** *How does boiling water move? (show demonstration) This is a group white board activity.*	**Main idea:** *Students will see colored paper movement in water and brain storm reason for movement*
	Unit Introduction: *Make foldable for definitions and drawings. Show powerpoint on Plate Tectonics.*	**Main idea:** *Students will be able to use foldable to quiz themselves and others*
	Level 1 Activities: *Odd Word Out activity on white boards and crossword puzzle* *In groups create hand symbols for each word and show another group the symbols* *Level 1 Assessment- highlight term that the student has not learned*	**Main idea:** *Recognition and analysis of word meaning* *Multi-intelligence learning* *Formative*
	Level 2 Activities: *Diagramming sheets for video and web presentation* *Pair and share ideas* *Liquids lab*	**Main idea:** Layer distinction Observe change in behavior with different liquid densities
	Level 3 Activities: *Plate Tectonics investigation plus questions* *Movie on Pacific Northwest*	*Plate boundary movements* *Pacific Norwest plate movement*
	Study Guide for all levels	
	Level 1, 2, 3 Assessment	
	Re-teach Session: *specialized for level needing the most reteaching*	
Teacher Resources: Curriculum, websites		

In the Unit Detail Section, an elicitation question starts each unit so the teacher can informally evaluate a student's prior knowledge or misconceptions about a topic or concept. Students get a chance to present their own thoughts and listen to others ideas.

Elicitation Question: An open ended question that piques student's interest.

White boarding is an engaging way for students to participate in the answering of an elicitation question. An example of an elicitation question for this unit is, "How does the boiling water move?" Students will need time to brainstorm in groups. They write their ideas on a white board. For fairness, students post them all at the same time.

After the elicitation question has been completed, teachers can evaluate whether students have any significant gaps that would require a change in the teaching plan. The elicitation question and any other introductory activities can be listed as an (I) in the level column of the unit guide for introductory.

The unit introduction can be an interesting conversation, movie, minilab or activity. The point of an introduction is to promote interest in a unit and familiarize the student with some parts of the unit. Both the elicitation question and the introduction have no grade assigned. They are strictly to create a buy-in for the student.

Teachers need to make clear to students what part of the rubric is being taught at the moment. **Students need to keep track and organize their work by levels**. Teachers should regularly check student's journals to see that students are organizing their journals by levels.

PARTS OF THE UNIT DETAIL MAP

Level 1 Activities

Recall and recognition are often used in activities for this level. Types of activities that fall into this low complexity of learning are:

➤ drawings of each of the vocabulary words
➤ definitions of each vocabulary word
➤ vocabulary crossword puzzles
➤ vocabulary matching
➤ vocabulary fill in the blank
➤ vocabulary games (i.e., Odd Word Out)
➤ dramatization of vocabulary
➤ vocabulary foldable

There are only four real considerations:
1) no knowledge outside of what is mentioned in the rubric for level 1 be used
2) all experiences at this point are lowest in complexity
3) all knowledge for this level must be foundational to the target
4) students should have a firm grasp of level 1 concepts before moving on to level 2 (formal assessment)

Level 2 Activities

Looking at the example rubric in Figure 9, the bridge knowledge links the vocabulary to the Plate Tectonic target. As a level 2 activity for the Plate Tectonic rubric, diagramming of convection currents adds a higher level of complexity to the learning.

A formative assessment should be given at this time to see if students are using level 1 knowledge properly in the level 2 activities.

It is important for the teacher to understand that each level (1 through 3) does not necessarily cover 33% of the information in a unit. That type of thinking is a carryover from the traditional averaging grading system. The only question students and teachers should be asking is a **yes** or **no** question. "Has the student shown enough evidence to prove they have mastered the learning in each level? " If the answer is **yes** then they are ready to go to the next level.

There are only three considerations that need to be met for level 2:
1) level 1 and 2 concepts listed on the rubric are the only concepts taught at this time
2) activities should be of intermediate complexity
3) level 2 is only formatively assessed

Level 3 Activities

Upper level Bloom's Taxonomy knowledge is usually proof of mastery at level 3.

Level 1 and 2 understanding is woven into level 3 understanding in the Plate Tectonic rubric, so when the teacher is communicating about level 3 information, level 1 and 2 are incorporated into the teaching and are then summatively assessed.

Level 4 Activities

Level 4 is the most complex unit. These activities go beyond the target. Not every student will be able to perform nor should be required to perform at level 4. In Figure 9, advanced learning comes in the form of predicting future tectonic movement. Predictions of this nature add a creative and evaluative component, producing an advanced target. Level 4 scaffold is addressed separately in this publication in Chapter 9, Advanced Learning.

Assessments

Assessments should reflect scaffolding similar to how assignments are layered. The main idea when scoring scaffold assessments is whether the student showed enough evidence of mastery. No percentages are involved in the score.

Assessment writing is possibly the weakest area in a teacher's educational preparation and yet it is one of the most important. Teachers are not usually formally trained for assessment construction. Without valid assessments, student mastery cannot really be determined. Assessments are discussed in more length later in the publication, in Chapter 7, Scaffold Assessment and Reflection.

Reteach Sessions

Reteach Session:
An alternative learning experience where students focus on problem areas where students are able to take another summative assessment to show mastery.

These sessions give students another opportunity at passing a summative assessment. Students that did not pass the first time will be pulled out and worked with separately, Chapter 8. Reteach sessions can be done at any level. It is up to the teacher to determine when and how often re-teaching is needed.

UNIT PLANNING GUIDE

The Unit Planning Guide Template allows for much more planning detail than the General Unit Map. The Unit Planning Guide begins the same as the General Unit Map. The state standard, target and rubric all are developed first and placed at the top of the lesson plan format. **The Unit Planning Template allows teachers to easily evaluate the lesson planning for rubric alignment.**

5 E Learning Cycle:
A learning cycle that helps teacher insures that a variety of learning is used in a unit.

The body of the Unit Planning Guide allows for the date of each lesson, 5E learning Cycle (Figure 10), rubric level content of each assignment and a description of the assignment. Teachers commonly have different lessons for different classes so there is a space available for the class period. When teachers take the time to list the rubric level for each assignment, a high degree of alignment occurs in the planning.

New to this format is the 5E Learning Cycle (Bybee 1989). This instructional model was originally designed as a teaching sequence to develop or enhance inquiry learning. For the following template, the 5E Learning Cycle is used only as a reminder to teachers to make sure they are using a variety of experiences in their lesson design. Each element of the learning cycle has been given a symbol (i.e., E1=Engagement). Midwestern State University has synthesized this model as:

Figure 10

5E Learning Cycle by Bybee

Engagement	Object, event or question used to engage students.
Exploration	Objects and phenomena are explored. Hands-on activities with guidance if needed.
Explanation	Students explain their understanding of concepts and processes.
Elaboration	Activities allow students to apply concepts in contexts, and build on or extend understanding and skill.
Evaluation	Students assess their knowledge, skills and abilities. Activities permit evaluation of student development and lesson effectiveness

(Midwestern State University an adaptation of Bybee 1989)

In the example below, much more specific information can be recorded for an individual teacher's records. The template for Unit Planning Guide (Figure 11) is in the Template Appendix.

Figure 11

Unit Planning Guide

Unit Planning Guide				
Content Area: *Earth Science*				
State Standard: *Draw a labeled diagram showing how convection in the upper mantle drives movement of crustal plates*				
Learning Target (s): *Students will be able to diagram events that occur at the plate boundaries including the boundaries of the Pacific Northwest* **Rubric Title:** *Plate Tectonics*				
Incomplete Evidence of Learning (I)	**Level 1** Foundational for Target	**Level 2** Progressing Toward Target Proficiency	**Level 3** Target Proficiency	**Level 4** Advanced Application of Target
	(lower level Bloom's) **I can …** • draw/define • crustal plates • crust • mantle • core • convection current	**(middle level Bloom's)** **I can…** *diagram the convection currents that drive crustal plates*	**(upper level Bloom's)** **I can…** *diagram events that occur at the plate boundaries including the boundaries of the Pacific Northwest*	**(high Bloom's)** **I can…** *predict how future movement of plates will change the shape/location of continents*

5-E Learning Cycle: **E1:** Engage   **E2:** Explore   **E3:** Explain   **E4:** Extend   **E5:** Evaluate

Date	5-E Learning Cycle	Rubric Level	Number of class periods	Activities:
	E1	I		*Elicitation Question-* How *does boiling water move? (show demonstration) This is a group white board activity*
	E2&3	1		*Make foldable for definitions and drawings. Show powerpoint on Plate Tectonics.*
	E4&3	1		*Odd Word Out activity on white boards and crossword puzzle*
	E1	1		*In groups create hand symbols for each word and show another group symbols*
	E5	1		*Level 1 Assessment- highlight terms that the student has not learned*
	E3	2		*Diagramming sheets for video and web presentation pair and share ideas*
	E1	2		*Liquids lab*
	E3	3		*Work sheet-Convection*
	E3	3		*Reading p245 and 246 with questions, pair and share answers*
	E3	3		*Plate Tectonics websites with notes*
		3		*Movie and notes*
	E1&3	3		*Plate Tectonic Investigation*
	E5	3		*Plate Tectonics Study Guide*
	E5	3		*Plate Tectonics Assessment*
	E5	3		*Reteach*
		1-3		

References:

Bybee, R.W. et al. (1989). *Science and technology education for the elementary years: Frameworks for curriculum and instruction.* Washington, D.C.: The National Center for Improving Instruction.

Midwestern State University Inquiry Approach, http://faculty.mwsu.edu/west/maryann.coe/coe/inquire/inquiry.htm

Office of Superintendent of Public Instruction, www.k12.wa.us

CHAPTER 4:
TYPES OF RUBRICS

There are three types of rubrics that will be discussed in this chapter: **Single Concept Rubric, Composite Rubric and Multitarget Rubric**

Guskey (2010) has separated learning goals into three groups, product, process and progress goals. A **process goal** defines desired classroom behaviors, not academic outcomes, so will not be addressed in this publication except for the Effort Reflection completed by the student after an assessment. **Product goals** are any targets that are meant to be assessed in any single period of time. Single Concept rubrics have product goals for targets.

Progress goals are targets that are assessed over a longer period of time. These goals can be assessed commonly to over the length of an entire year. Progress is assessed through out the year but mastery is not expected until the end of the year. Multitarget rubric and composite rubrics have targets that can be both product and progress related goals.

SINGLE CONCEPT RUBRIC

The single concept rubric is the most commonly used in the classroom. A single concept rubric has one target that is the learning goal. Typically, a student will be assessed on a target at the end of a unit. The single concept rubric has been the main focus of chapters 2-3. The following (Figure 12) is an example of a single concept rubric.

Figure 12

Use of the Writing Process Rubric

Learning Target Levels	I Incomplete No Evidence Learning	Level 1 Foundation for Meeting Target	Level 2 Progressing Towards Target	Level 3 Meets Target
Performance Description	No evidence of meeting standard.	I can define the following: • Draft • Graphic organizer • Revise • Edit	I can produce a draft of using my graphic organizer	I can revise and edit to improve my draft

COMPOSITE RUBRIC

The rubric (Figure 13) below is an example of a composite rubric, where the rubric is given at the end of several single concept targets to tie them all together.

Composite Rubric: A rubric that is the culmination of several rubrics.

The same rules apply for a single concept rubric, composite rubric or any other rubric. Foundational learning comes first at level 1, then bridge knowledge, level 2, then the complete target, level 3.

For this composite rubric, students went through several units starting with a unit to learn how to construct a data table from a scenario. Once students were proficient at constructing data tables, the teacher presented the next unit, constructing graphs from data tables. Once constructing graphs were mastered, the Connecting Data Tables, Graphs and Equations Rubric was taught.

Figure 13

Connecting Data Tables, Graphs and Equations Rubric

Incomplete No Evidence About Target Understanding	Level 1 Foundational Learning for Target	Level 2 Progressing Toward Target	Level 3 Meeting Target	Level 4 Advanced Application of Target
No or little work completed to show understanding	I can read a scenario construct a data table.	I can construct a corresponding graph from the data table.	I can construct a corresponding equation from a graph.	I can describe the relationship of two graphs.

MULTITARGET RUBRIC

Multitarget Rubric:
Several related rubrics that are used over a long period of time.

A multitarget rubric (progress goals) is used when a teacher has a set of targets that will be applied over a period of time. The multitarget rubric is useful in journal assessments further discussed in Chapter 5.

The example below (Figure 14) is a health and fitness multitarget rubric.

State Standard: The student demonstrates manipulative skills with stationary and moving targets in group activities.

Figure 14

Volleyball Rubric

Rubric Title	Level 1 Foundational Learning for Target	Level 2 Progressing Toward Target	Level 3 Meeting Target
Serving a volleyball	I can use the proper form when serving	I can serve the ball underhand over the net	I can serve the ball overhand over the net
Setting a volleyball	I can set the ball to myself	I can set the ball that a team mate tosses to me	I can set the ball when it is returned to me from the other side of the net
Hitting a volleyball	I can pass the ball to myself in practice	I can hit the ball that a team mate tosses to me	I can hit the ball when it is returned to me from the other side of the net

The composite rubric above will be used during unit of volleyball. In the case of physical fitness where students usually don't have journals or binders to refer to the rubric, it may be necessary to make a large poster of the rubric so students can evaluate their own skill level through out the volleyball unit.

Notice that the multitarget rubric does not have a level 4 associated with it. It is possible to add a level 4 with a multitarget rubric. However, some targets do not lend themselves well for additional advanced achievement target construction. They simply lack advanced progression.

RUBRICS FOR GRADE DETERMINATION

| Grade Determination Rubrics: Rubrics that are used to formulate a letter grade. |

It is possible to confuse a grade determination rubric with a target rubric. The end of grading period rubric is used to produce a single grade on a report card. When assigning a grade for a report card, a rubric is needed to establish an A, B, C, D, I or F. This is important to communicate to students and parents.

Target indicators (figure 15) speak to a specific knowledge that the student must master.

Figure 15

Target Indicators

Incomplete No Evidence About Target Understanding	Level 1 Foundational Learning for Target	Level 2 Progressing Toward Target	Level 3 Meeting Target	Level 4 Advanced Application of Target

The language for indicators for a grade determination rubric (Figure 16) is various and not usually scaffold like a target rubric. These rubrics are divided into levels more subjectively, rather than descriptively like a target rubric. Guskey (2010) lists many indicators for student performance.

An example of grade creation indicators is shown below.

Figure 16

Grade Indicators

Level 1 Rarely Met Standard	Level 2 Occasionally Met Standard	Level 3 Frequently Met Standard	Level 4 Consistently Met Standard

These are indicators reflecting the trend of target scores for a particular class over a grading period. These indicators blend the actual target scores into one singular grade. Since this type of rubric does not contain language specific to a target scaffolding, it is not appropriate for single concept, composite or multitarget rubrics.

References:

Guskey, Thomas R., Bailey, Jane M., (2010). *Developing Standards-Based Report Cards.* Thousand Oaks, CA: Corwin

Office of Superintendent of Public Instruction, www.k12.wa.us

CHAPTER 5:
ORGANIZATION OF A STUDENT JOURNAL

Journaling is one of the most powerful learning instruments that the teacher and student have to monitor progression of learning. From beginning to end, the student virtually creates an account of the students learning path.

Journaling is one of the most powerful learning instruments that the teacher and student have to monitor progression of learning.

A journal can include:
- Details, facts and key concepts
- Reflections and questions about learning
- Notes and revisions
- Reading segments
- Graphic organizers
- Diagrams and descriptions
- Targets and rubrics
- Research, projects and lab write ups

Student journals can be used for formative or summative assessments. In essence, the journal is a real time record of all activities that document the progression of student thinking and learning toward target mastery.

There are many learning mechanisms that can help capture student learning in a student journal. Once captured, the student will be able to review, monitor and reflect on their own student's learning progress. Formative assessments should be kept and organized in each journal so students can see progress in their learning.

The journal can also be a place for more creative student expression, including stories, booklets, and pamphlets, foldables and even pop-ups.

A standard set up for a notebook should be:

1) Title page: students write their class period, name and teachers name on the page so it can be easily returned if lost. Also, the student should be encouraged to draw and color this page to promote ownership of the journal.

2) Table of Contents: all assignment dates, titles and pages the rubric level for each are listed in the proper order by date.

3) Paginated Pages: all pages should match the numbers listed in the table of contents.

4) Heading of Each Page: all headings should match the titles in the table of contents.

Coloring rubric column by levels helps students see level pattern. Any color pattern can be used. A stop light pattern is easy to remember.

It is helpful to make a poster for easy reference.

Red- Level 1
Yellow-Level 2
Green- Level 3

Once the rubric is color coded, the same can be done for the level listing in the table of contents. Students can easily identify what to study for each assignment by examining the table of contents.

Figure 17

Table of Contents Example

Table of Contents

Date	Level	Assignment Name	Page #	Score
3/7	I	Mineral or Rock?	28	
3/8	I	Rock Cycle	29	
3/8	1	Rock Cycle Vocabulary	29	
3/8	1	Rock Cycle Big Picture	30	
3/9	1	Rock Cycle Foldable	31	
3/12	1	Rock Cycle Level 1 Quiz	32	Pass
3/13	2	Rock Cycle Graphic Organizer	33	
3/14	2	Computer Activity on Rocks	34	
3/15	2	Rock Laboratory	35-36	
3/16	2	Rock Lab Quiz-Level 2	37	Pass
3/19	3	Rock Cycle Movie Notes	38	
3/20	3	Rock Cycle Handout	39	
3/21	3	Story of Rocky Rock	40-42	Pass
3/24	3	Rock Cycle Study Guide	43	
3/25	1-3	Rock Cycle Assessment	44-45	

I = Introductory Material

It is easy to see from the example table of contents above (Figure 17) that students will readily find each level for any future studying needs.

Notice that every assignment is not graded. It is only necessary to indicate "pass' for the formative assessments in the journal.

JOURNAL ASSESSMENT

As importantly as organizing information around new content, journals also show a student's diagramming, graphing and data table construction abilities. Diagramming, graphing and data table construction can be assessed if there is a content target for each.

Here are two examples of state standards that can support journal assessment:
- Collecting, analyzing and displaying data or writing
- Communicating results using pictures, tables, charts, graphic displays and text that are clear, accurate and informative

Student thinking is easily communicated through their journal, as well as mastery of concepts.

Many contents will have a standard for which a journal target can be crafted.

The journal assessment rubric below is a multitarget rubric. In a multitarget rubric, the teacher chooses which of the targets out of the journal rubric will be used to evaluate the student journal in that grading period. This target is then clearly communicated to the student and taught by the teacher. It is possible that the teacher will evaluate all the targets in the rubric. When multiple targets are evaluated, students should be encouraged to use and maintain older targets while new targets are assigned.

Figure 18 is an example of a multitarget journal rubric. The teacher can decide to evaluate one to three different attributes of a student journal.

The journal assessment and reflection example below (figure 18) can be changed to add any number of journal targets. Both the student and the teacher evaluate the target achievement for the journal.

After the reflection has been completed by the student and the teacher, the student can create a plan to improve or maintain their journal. Taking the time to evaluate a student journal is a key factor for student improvement of their ability to organize both thoughts and work. By both the teacher and the student reflecting on the journal targets, teachers can have an open and informative conversation with students about journal attributes and improvements.

Figure 18

Journal Multitarget Assessment Rubric and Reflection Example

Level	1	2	3
Using diagrams, tables and graphs to communicate ideas	Diagram labeling is relevant to target understanding	Caption of diagram is relevant to target understanding	Diagram shows an understanding of target
Understanding of target	Provides a general understanding of target	Provides examples of target	Provides understanding of details of target
Conclusion writing	Gives a general statement for a conclusion	Restates data in conclusion	Explains how the data supports the general statement

Target(s) that will be assessed are: conclusion writing

Student Reflection:
My assessment of my journal is **level**...*2*
Because: I gave a description what <u>taxes</u> *are used to create public schools and state parks. I showed tax totals to support my idea but I did not explain how the taxes are separated for each.*
Teacher Reflection:
Assessment of this student journal is **level**...*2*
Because*: Missing the level 3 support statement*

My plan to improve or maintain journal is:
Finish level 3 Conclusion and make sure I understand what it is

CHAPTER 6:
STUDENT RETRIEVAL OF SCAFFOLD LEARNING

In Standard Based Teaching, all activities including assessments and study guides must be aligned with the rubric.

There is a very diverse group of activities that teachers use label 'study guides'. When searching the web, study guides fall into three groups:

- A list of targets or contents that will be covered on the assessment
- A set of problems of the type that will be covered on the assessment
- A list of essential questions that prompt the student to evaluate the appropriate content

According to David Sousa (2001) in *How the Brain Learns,* learning and retrieval mechanisms are different. The brain constantly works to seek patterns so it may create meaning from information. We store information by recognizing similarities in the information while retrieving information by differences. Reviewing information by levels is consistent with retrieving information by differences.

In standard based teaching, the study guide must have the same organizational structure as the rubric. Sousa calls this *chunking,* where information is stored in a few larger blocks rather in multiple small blocks of information.

Strategic Study Guide: Study guides that help students diagnose what information has been mastered.

In addition to using learning levels in a study guide, the study guide must have other important features. It should help students to evaluate what has been learned and what the student will do for additional learning. These three elements make a **strategic study guide.**

GUIDELINES FOR A STRATEGIC STUDY GUIDE

Study guides, while keeping in line with the rubric, should do three things:

- State **what** must be learned for the assessment
- Be diagnostic so the student can **determine what has not been mastered**
- List a menu of activities students may choose regarding **how** students can learn levels they have missed on the study guide

In the example below (Figure 19), the rubric and study guide have been aligned. Each level is addressed in the study guide.

Students may determine surface area by calculating the area of the faces and adding the results.

Figure 19

Surface Area Rubric

Level 1 Foundation for Target	Level 2 Progressing Toward Target Proficiency	Level 3 Target Proficiency
I can define/draw an example of the following: • cm • cm2 • length of a rectangular prism • height of a rectangular prism • width of a rectangular prism • faces of a prism	I can calculate: a. the front of a rectangular prism b. the top of a rectangular prism c. the side of a rectangular prism	I can add up all the sides to find the surface area of a rectangular prism

In the rubric above (Figure 19), for level 1 there is a list of concepts the student needs to be able to define and/or draw.

Drawing a concept or visualized note taking will help the teacher evaluate if a student can transfer the knowledge to an image, a more complex level of understanding. Visualized note-taking uses both sides of our brain and increases the possibility that the knowledge will be learned (Sousa 2001).

For level 2 the front, top and side of a rectangular prism must be calculated. For level 3 all the calculations must be added up to produce the surface area for the prism.

Each level has a discrete set of learning and should be taught in that progression. The study guide should reflect that exact scaffolding.

Looking at the study guide for this rubric (figure 20), it follows the Guidelines for a Strategic Study Guide.
1) All three levels are represented in the study problems
2) Students are asked to diagnose if they can complete the study guide correctly without assistance
3) Students are asked to make a plan about what they are going to do if they do not understand

It is important that after the teacher reviews the answer with students, that students implement their plan to learn unlearned material.

Figure 20
Study Guide for Surface Area of a Rectangular Prism

Study Guide Name: Surface Area of a Rectangular Prism

Level 1: *(general description)*

Define and draw the following:

	Define:	Draw:
○ cm ○ cm2 ○ length of a rectangular prism ○ height of a rectangular prism ○ width of a rectangular prism ○ faces of a prism		

Level 2: *(general description)*

Calculate the length, height and width of this prism. Show all work.

5 cm

3 cm

4 cm

Level 3: *(general description)*

Calculate the surface area of the rectangular prism above.

　○　I can complete level 1 without assistance

　○　I can complete level 2 without assistance

　○　I can complete level 3 without assistance

If I cannot complete each level without assistance, I plan to (circle one):
Ask the teacher for help, ask a friend for help, review work from my journal or_____.

Directly after an assessment has been given, students should evaluate how well they feel they have learned assessment material. Once students evaluate their learning, it is important that they also evaluate the amount of effort they spent studying for an assessment. Marzano (2001) reports that effort is correlative to achievement. This comes as no surprise to educators but may be a new idea for the student. **Students need to reflect on their effort so they can better correlate what they do with how well they learn.**

In *Motivating Students to Learn* by Brophy (2004), students can be taught to increase effort and thereby increase achievement. In figure 21, Effort and Achievement Reflection Rubric Example, students evaluate the effort they have put into learning. Students can then evaluate their achievement level by their effort output.

This is the best time for a teacher to discuss with a student that the effort the student is putting forth may need to increase to increase the amount of learning.

Figure 21

Effort and Achievement Reflection Rubric Example

	Effort Reflection		Achievement Reflection
3	I worked to understand what was taught by asking questions when stuck, completing assignments in class, studying for the assessment	3	I used my study guide to assess what I learned, I can prove I can understand level 3
2	I worked to complete work and understand what was taught but I did not always stay focused, review work or ask questions	2	I used my study guide to assess what I learned, I can prove I can understand level 2
1	I put some effort into my journal but I did not understand what was taught	1	I used my study guide to assess what I learned, I can prove I can understand level 1
I	I have not put effort into my learning	I	I did not understand the study guide

(I= Incomplete effort or achievement)

Assessment Name:
Assessment Score:

Post Assessment Reflection:
I can explain my:

Assessment score and **effort** reflection:

Assessment score and **achievement** reflection:

Goal Setting
Effort Goal for next assessment:

How I will reach my effort goal:

Achievement Goal for next assessment:

How I will reach my achievement goal:

The Effort and Achievement Reflection rubric is filled out after completing the study guide. **The effort rubric is a process rubric and so the indicators are set up differently.** These indicators are more reflective of the quality of work the student is doing.

Once a student gets their assessment score back, they load the score in the assessment section of the rubric. The student fills out the Post Assessment Reflection where students analyze their score and correlate it to the effort and achievement information they have previously submitted.

Teacher's conferencing with students helps the student become aware of their efforts when confronted with low achievement scores. If a student scores low on an assessment and marks high on effort then the teacher should discuss what the student is spending effort doing that is not helping their achievement. The student may need to be taught more efficient studying methods.

If the student scores low on an assessment and also marks a low effort score then the teacher should discuss why more effort should be given when studying for an assessment.

Reference:

Brophy, J. E. (2005), Motivating Students to Learn. Psychology Press

Guskey, Thomas R., Bailey, Jane M., (2010). *Developing Standards-Based Report Cards.* Thousand Oaks, CA: Corwin

Marzano, R. J., Pickering, D.J., Pollock, J.E. (2005). *Classroom Instruction That Works.* Pearson Education, Inc., New Jersey

Sousa, D. A. (2nd Ed). (2001) *How the Brain Learns.* Crowin Press, Thousand Oaks, California

Office of Superintendent of Public Instruction, www.k12.wa.us

CHAPTER 7:
SCAFFOLD ASSESSMENT AND REFLECTION

Assessment construction is the area of teacher preparation most neglected by universities, districts and teachers alike. Equally neglected is training regarding assessment analysis of student data. Teachers construct assessments with the best intentions of creating a tool that can accurately evaluate what students learn. However, without proper training on assessments construction, assessments can lack reliability and validity.

In the standard based teaching system of learning, the assessments mirror rubrics and study guides. This complete alignment adds reliability and validity to each assessment (Moskal and Leydens 2000). An example of this alignment is seen in figure 22, the Layers of the Earth assessment.

Typically, Level 1 is usually assessed by requiring the student to define and/or diagram the unit vocabulary. In the Layers of the Earth rubric, students use vocabulary to identify each layer in a diagram rather than defining each word.

Levels 2 and 3 incorporate the Layers of the Earth vocabulary and require the student to add more information showing a deeper understanding of each Earth layer.

Figure 22

Layers of the Earth Rubric

Incomplete No Evidence About Standard Understanding (I)	Level 1 Foundational Learning for Target	Level 2 Progressing Toward Target	Level 3 Meeting Target
	I can **identify** the following layers of the Earth: Crust Mantle Inner Core Outer Core	I can give the **thickness** for each layer of the Earth	I can describe the **chemical nature** of each layer of the Earth

Using the rubric above, the Earth Layers assessment would look like this:

Figure 23

Earth Layers Assessment Example

Level 1: I can **identify** the layers of the Earth in the diagram below.

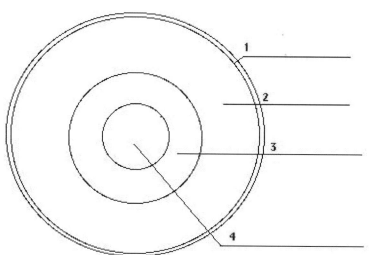

Diagram not drawn to scale

Level 2: I can give the **thickness** for each layer of the Earth.

1.

2.

3.

4.

Level 3: I can describe the **chemical nature** of each layer of the Earth.

1.

2.

3.

4.

In the assessment in Figure 23, each level is identified. Student read the description statement from each level. This reinforces the importance of rubric familiarity for each student.

Another example of assessment alignment with rubric language can be seen in Figures 24 and 25. Fourth grade students are assessed on sentence construction.

Figure 24

Sentence Construction Rubric

Incomplete No Evidence About Standard Understanding (I)	Level 1 Foundational Learning for Target	Level 2 Progressing Toward Target	Level 3 Meeting Target
	I can give an **example** of : **Capitalizing Punctuation**	I can **write** sentences that begin with **capital letters**	I can **write** sentences using the **proper punctuation**

The level expectations are clearly stated and each assessment question is aligned with the rubric.

The assessment for the Sentence Construction Rubric could look like Figure 25 below.

Figure 25

Sentence Construction Assessment Example

Level 1:
*I can **give an example** of capitalization:*
    Capitalize each:
    1. dog _____
    2. worm _____
    3. door _____

*I can give **three examples** of punctuation:*
    1. _____
    2. _____
    3. _____

Level 2:
*I can write sentences that begin with **capital letters**.*
    Capitalize each sentence.
    1. my family went to the park.

    2. i can't wait to go to the movie!

    3. can you help me swim?

Level 3:
*I can write a sentence using the **proper punctuation**.*
    Add the proper punctuation for each sentence:

    1. When are we going fishing

    2. My favorite sport is soccer

    3. Wow, you really scared me

POST ASSESSMENT REFLECTION

The Effort and Achievement Reflection Rubric from Chapter 6, provides a tool for students to evaluate their effort and achievement level that helps students determine their assessment readiness.

Students fill out the first part of the template (Figure 26) before they take the assessment.

Figure 26

Effort and Achievement Reflection Rubric Example

	Effort Reflection		Achievement Reflection
3	I worked to understand what was taught by asking questions when stuck, completing assignments in class, studying for the assessment	3	Using my study guide to assess what I learned, I can prove I can understand level 3
2	I worked to complete work and understand what was taught but I did not always stay focused, review work or ask questions	2	Using my study guide to assess what I learned, I can prove I can understand level 2
1	I put some effort into my journal but I did not understand what was taught	1	Using my study guide to assess what I learned, I can prove I can understand level 1
I	I have not put effort into my learning	I	I did not understand the study guide

(I= Incomplete effort or achievement)

After the assessment has been taken and scored, the student completes the rest of the template, the Post Assessment Reflection (Figure 27).

Figure 27

Post Assessment and Reflection

| Assessment Name: |
| Assessment Score: |

Post Assessment Reflection:
I can explain:
- How my assessment score relates to my **effort** reflection:

- How my assessment score relates to my **achievement** reflection:

Goal Setting
- **Effort Goal** for next assessment:

- How I will reach my effort goal:

- **Achievement Goal** for next assessment:

- How I will reach my achievement goal:

The student copies their score in the space for assessment score and then completes the rest of the form. **This reflection helps students to make a correlation between their assessment score, effort and actual achievement.** The teacher and the student now have an opportunity to deeply engage about student effort. This template can help the student to recognize they are not putting enough effort or properly studying for an assessment.

Brophy (2005) believes that this type of honest evaluation, where effort is linked to achievement is one of the few ways to change student behavior regarding low achievement. Helping students change from nonparticipants into active learners is difficult but

This gives the teacher and the student the opportunity to thoroughly discuss whether the student is studying or completing the work needed to achieve target proficiency.

tools like this can help make a difference.

References:

Brophy, J. E. (2005), *Motivating Students to Learn.* Psychology Press

Moskal, Barbara M., Leydens, Jon A. (2000). Scoring rubric development: validity and reliability. *Practical Assessment, Research & Evaluation*, 7(10).

Sousa, D. A. (2nd Ed). (2001) *How the Brain Learns*. Crowin Press, Thousand Oaks, California

CHAPTER 8:
RETEACH SESSION USING A RUBRIC SCAFFOLD

WHAT IS RETEACH?

If students are not successful in passing their summative assessment, they should be given another chance to gain mastery of the target. There are a multitude of reasons why students do not pass a summative assessment. Regardless of why students do not pass the first time, those students will need structured time and attention to reach mastery. Providing students with an effective reteach session when they have not reached target proficiency, underscores the importance of learning to the student. Students often are appreciative of this second chance.

> Reteach sessions should be considered by the student as a way to achieve learning, not a punishment.

It is helpful if two or more teachers are sharing students when reteaching. One teacher works with the students who need the reteaching while the other teacher conducts an enrichment activity with the students who have already mastered the target. It is also possible to get help from other staff, librarians or educational assistants if no other teacher is available.

If there is no other teacher to help manage reteaching, students can work on enrichment activities in the same classroom with students who are participating in reteach.

Reteach sessions are only successful if the teacher presents them positively to the student and not punitively. **Reteach sessions should be considered by the student as a way to improve achievement, not a punishment.**

WHY RETEACH?

Ruby Payne (2005) states that students of generational poverty speak in a causal register, a cultural and social sub-set of formal language. Classroom and state assessments are written in a formal register. Speaking in a causal register, Payne says that these students typically only have a vocabulary of 400-500 words. By the time a student reaches high school, they are potentially missing thousands of words in their vocabulary.

Casual register sentences are usually incomplete. Also, there is a custom of using body language to communicate instead of words. Formal register on the other hand, is characterized by a large vocabulary set, complete sentences and highly structured word choice and use.

> Students that can not acquire an understanding for the formal register system of speaking lag behind in achievement.

Students that do not communicate in formal register lag behind in achievement. Further, because state assessments are written in a formal register, students perform poorly on these assessments. It is absolutely necessary for these students to get assistance so they may master the formal register.

Since level 1 is primarily vocabulary, it may be necessary that these students pass level 1 before proceeding further. Giving students another opportunity to master the target will help close the learning gap for students of poverty and other under performing students.

Reteach sessions are important for contents that do not lend themselves to repeated summative assessments of the same target. Math is a content that may have several opportunities to assess per target. Reteach for math or other such subjects may not be necessary if teachers are already intervening with students that are performing poorly.

However, many contents will have only one summative per target. Without reteach sessions, students who cannot pass the summative assessment the first time will have no other opportunity to show they have target mastery.

HOW RETEACH WORKS

Reteach is a very simple concept. Once a student fails a final or summative assessment, an alternative learning experience is scheduled. A decision must be made as to what level should be taught. If a significant number of students failed level 1, then this problem should be addressed before moving to a higher level.

Since level 1 is usually vocabulary building, teaching student's effective ways to study and learn by rote is a good reteaching strategy.

Diagramming can help students to synthesis information in a unique way so more memory pathways are developed.

In the following example (Figure 28), level 1 definitions are given to students then they are asked to create a diagram for each. Diagramming can help students to synthesize information in a unique way so denser memory pathways are developed (Sousa 2001). Ultimately this type of conceptual activity helps create a deeper understanding.

In the beginning of the reteach session for level 1, students are given a check off list and the definitions that must be learned. A study partner is assigned. Each student quizzes the other on the list of words. Each student must go over the list several times. When students miss a definition, the quizzing student states the definition. The student who is being quizzed then repeats the definition. The student is doing the quizzing comes back to that definition later and asks it again.

Reteach can be conducted with any study method the teacher believes is an effective way for students to engage in learning.

Figure 28

Level 1 Reteach

Vocabulary Terms	Definition	Quiz another (check off when done)	You are quizzed (check off when done)
Sum	The final number from adding		
Subtract	finding how many are left when a number of items are taken away		
Add	finding the total number of items		
Plus	(+) means to add		
Minus	(-) means to subtract		

Trial assessment:

Vocabulary Terms	Definition for each:
Sum	
Subtract	
Add	
Plus	
Minus	

Ready to take the assessment?

After students quiz each other, a formative assessment is taken to see if the student is ready for the summative assessment. This template used for level 1 reteach can be found in the List of Templates in the Appendix.

For levels 2 and 3, a different tack must be taken. These levels involve deeper thinking. Reteach for level 2 or 3 is less formulaic than level 1 so analysis of level 2 and 3 concepts is necessary.   It is important to make sure that the heart of the concept being assessed is the focus of the reteach. Diagramming combined with strategic questions help teachers and students determine if the student is ready to take the reteach assessment.

 Other methods may include having the student complete a graphic organizer with the important information or reviewing provided examples to detect content errors.

Glaser (1988) observes that at first, student knowledge is shallow but as learning progresses, students connect chunks of knowledge creating a deeper more comprehensive understanding. If a student is not successful at stringing together chunks or concepts, gaps can occur. Fogarty (1994) observes that once gaps occur in student learning, it is necessary for students to recognize those gaps so they can link their previous knowledge to new concepts before mastery can occur.

Using graphic organizers or diagramming as a reteach strategy helps reveal gaps in student learning and provides a vehicle to learning missing knowledge. An example of this can be found in the following social studies standard in Figure 29.

Write a conclusion on how two groups made cultural contributions to your community or the world by comparing the contributions of each cultural group with one similarity and difference.

Figure 29

Cultural Groups in Community Rubric

Incomplete Evidence of Learning (I)	Level 1 Foundational for Target	Level 2 Progressing Toward Target Proficiency	Level 3 Target Proficiency
	(lower level Bloom's) I can define... • Cultural • Community • Contribution • Conclusion • Groups in a community	(middle level Bloom's) I can... *list similarities and differences between two or more cultural groups in my community*	(upper level Bloom's) I can... *write a conclusion about how two cultural groups contribute to the my community*

In Figure 30, a graphic organizer is used for the level 2 reteach session: *list similarities and differences between two or more cultural groups in my community.*

Figure 30   **Level 2 Cultural Groups Reteach**

Name _____   Subject: <u>Social Studies</u>

Teacher: Date: _____

Level 2: Cultural Groups in Community

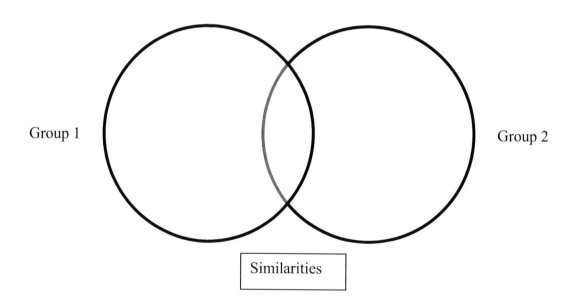

Group 1   Group 2

Similarities

A different graphic organizer below (Figure 31) is used for the level 3 reteach session: *write a conclusion about how two cultural groups contribute to my community.*

Figure 31

Level 3 Cultural Groups Reteach

Characteristics of group 1	Characteristics of group 2

Ways in which cultural groups 1 and 2 are alike:
Ways in which cultural groups 1 and 2 are different:
How do these cultural groups contribute to the community:

By diagramming concepts from each level in a graphic organizer, students and teachers can recognize gaps in learning. Once the student and teacher have identified these gaps, strict attention can be paid to those areas of learning in the reteach session.

A different approach for level 2 and 3 reteach sessions can be seen in the example below (figure 32). In this example of the reteach format, students answer questions about a particular concept in a before and after context of a reteach session.

Figure 32

Example of Reteach for levels 2 and 3.

Before Reteach Session   **After Reteach Session**

What are the similarities and differences of two cultural groups in our community?	What are the similarities and differences of cultural two groups in our community?

- o I shared my differences with my partner.
- o My partner explained her/his differences to me.
- o I explained my differences to the teacher.

In this type of reteach format **the student can see clearly that they have progressed.**

References:

Fogarty, R. (1994) *How To Teach For Metacognition*. Palatine,Ill: IRI/Skylight.

Glaser, R. (1988). *Cognitive science and education.* Cognitive Science Journal, 115, 22-44.

Office of Superintendent of Public Instruction, www.k12.wa.us

Payne, R. K. (1998/2005). *A Framework for understanding poverty* (4th ed.). Highlands, TX: RFT Publishing.

Sousa, D. A. (2nd Ed). (2001) *How the Brain Learns*. Crowin Press, Thousand Oaks, California

CHAPTER 9:
ADVANCED LEARNING

We are responsible as educators to teach all students in our classrooms. This includes the advanced student. These students may already know much of what the teacher is introducing to the class. If they do not know the concepts, they may learn those concepts quickly. Often these students sit with little to do in a classroom while waiting for the rest of the class to catch up. Advanced students will learn less than the rest of the students unless advanced work is provided for them.

It is difficult to find a clear definition of advanced thinking for students in the classroom. There is not a clear agreement among teachers, state documents and gifted experts as to the definition of an advanced student. It makes sense that advanced learning should incorporate the highest level of Blooms Taxonomy, evaluation and creativity.

Advanced thinking in the classroom should also be associated with autonomous research and reflection. It should be associated with critical thinking as well. According to Ennis (1992), critical thinking is defined as "reasonable, reflective thinking focused on deciding what to believe and do."

For the leading public universities (Geiser 2004), these advanced students show that they can challenge themselves by taking more rigorous coursework. They are seen as more highly qualified and desired students than those who have not.

Furthermore, it has been well documented that there is a distinct underrepresentation of lower socioeconomic and racial/ethnic students in honors or AP courses where advanced learning occurs. Therefore, there is a need to present advanced learning and thinking opportunities in the regular classroom.

This type of higher level thinking should be integrated in America's schools from kindergarten to 12th grade to ensure as many students are qualified for post high school education as possible. However, asking teachers merely to 'go beyond the target' is vague and directionless. The teacher should look to their state standards for ideas about how to address advanced thinking in the classroom. There may be descriptors that teachers can use to create a level 4 scaffold. Examples of state 4th grade reading performance descriptors for proficient and advanced language can be seen below.

Advanced students are often sitting with little to do in classroom, waiting for the rest of the class to finish. This is the perfect time for these students to work on advanced concepts. The teacher provides these exercises in a designated place in the classroom, requiring a certain amount to be completed at the end of a grading period. Then if students have difficulties they can ask for help.

Figure 33

Proficient and Advanced 4th Grade Reading Skill Characteristics

Proficient Reading Skill Characteristics

• Students appropriately read for comprehension, analysis, and evaluation.
• Students read fluently, with accuracy, expression, and appropriate rate.
• Students demonstrate understanding of themes, main ideas, and details by using documented evidence from text.
• Students have multiple strategies for understanding unknown words.
• Students can read a variety of materials including charts, graphs, and captions to deepen or confirm their knowledge.
• Students are able to use text features such as headings to quickly find the answer to a question or a specific spot in the text.
• Students can re-tell a story explaining characters and plot, emphasizing the most important parts without getting lost in the details.
• Students can give opinions about the story and support those opinions with details.
• Students can identify and understand important facts and organize them into meaning. Students know and use the way a book is organized by using the table of contents, index, glossary, headings, captions, and additional text features.
• Students can use information from their reading to explain what they have learned or what new thing they would do.
• Students refer to text as a resource to help them find answers, analyze, make inferences, and use their own knowledge to construct their own meaning.

Advanced Reading Skill Characteristics

• Students read deeply for comprehension, analysis, and evaluation.
• Students read fluently, with accuracy, expression, and appropriate rate on a wide range of texts and genres.
• Students have the ability to skim and scan text for a specific purpose.
• Students demonstrate a strong understanding of themes, main ideas and details by using well-documented evidence from text.
• Students have multiple strategies for understanding unknown words.
• Students can read a variety of materials including charts, graphs, and captions to deepen or confirm their knowledge.
• Students are able to use text features to quickly find the answer to a question or a specific spot in the text.
• Students can re-tell a story explaining characters and plot, emphasizing the most important parts without getting lost in the details.
• Students are highly motivated and strongly self-directed and "read to learn".
• Students have a wide range of metacognitive strategies to aid in comprehension and analysis, and always persevere with difficult text.

Looking more closely at language from Figure 33, it is easy to see there is very little overlap between some standards of proficient and advanced learning. Some of the language is the same for proficient (level 3) and advanced learning (level 4). However, some of the language is completely unique to the advanced level of learning. Level 4 is always more complex than level 3.

Level 3: Proficient Learning states that:
Students refer to text as a resource to help them find answers, analyze, make inferences, and use their own knowledge to construct their own meaning.

Level 4: Advanced Learning states that:
Students have a wide range of metacognitive strategies to aid in comprehension and analysis, and always persevere with difficult text.

This divergence in descriptors from level 3 to level 4 will help teachers to construct assignments that meet level 4 achievement.

If state standards are not available for advanced learning descriptors, **teachers can construct their own advanced targets using the guidelines below.**

When constructing advanced achievement targets:
- Do not add difficulty without adding complexity in learning.
- Using a higher level Bloom's taxonomy than the level 3 target will increase complexity
- Adding content outside the level 3 target will increase complexity
- Sometimes simply changing the perspective in diagramming, writing or problem solving can add complexity

Figure 34

Rational Numbers Rubric

Learning Target Levels	(I) Incomplete Preparation	Level 1 Foundation for Meeting Target	Level 2 Progressing Towards Target	Level 3 Meets Target	Level 4 Meets Target
Performance Description	No evidence of meeting standard.	Using whole numbers, I can graph both negative and positive numbers on a number line	Using decimals, I can graph both negative and positive numbers on a number line	Using fractions, I can graph both negative and positive numbers on a number line	I can convert irrational numbers to rational number and graph on a number line

In the rubric above (Figure 34), student should be able to graph negative and positive fractions on a number line. To add complexity, the advanced learning level asks students to convert irrational numbers to rational numbers then graph the newly converted rational number. There are two new additions to this level than goes beyond the target learning in this example. First, the student must learn about irrational numbers. Second, the student must learn to convert an irrational number to a rational number.

Once a level 4 concept has been constructed or identified, the teacher may choose to give this as an independent study where students will be given an assessment as an addendum to the regularly assessed target **or** as a project grade that is collected at a particular time.

This level of learning should always be considered 'beyond' the regular target. **Students should self-select to participate in advanced learning activities.**

Since students self-select working beyond the target, it is important that the teacher be available for assistance if a student gets stuck. The teacher should not give students the answers but direct them by asking a series of inquiry questions or providing a resource that will help the student work through the difficult nature of the questions.

Because this level is advanced, only students that have the upper thinking skills will be able to complete it. Many students will not be able to satisfactorily complete this level.

In Figure 35 and 36 is an example of level 3 and 4 for diagramming a heart.

Figure 35

Level 3 Diagramming of the Heart

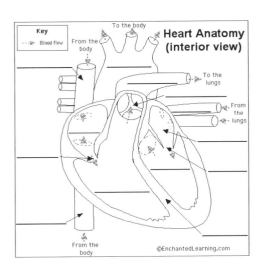

Figure 36

Level 4 Diagramming of the Heart

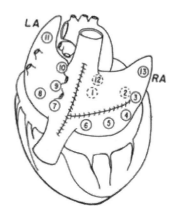

In the above figures 35 and 36, complexity is added simply by changing the perspective of the diagram. Figure 35 is a very common view of the heart. This perspective is found on may websites and science texts.

Figure 36 has a very different perspective. By simply shifting the angle the heart is viewed by, insert an advanced element is into the diagramming.

With practice, teachers can have a menu of advanced work for students to complete in their classes.

References:

Ennis, R. (1992). *Critical thinking: What is it?* Proceedings of the 48th Annual Meeting of the Philosophy of Education Society, Denver, Colorado, March 27-30.

Geiser, Saul. Santelices, Veronica. (2004). *The Role of Advanced Placement and Honors Courses in College Admissions*, CSHE.4.04. (2004) University of California, Berkeley

Office of Superintendent of Public Instruction, www.k12.wa.us

Oxford Journals Medicine Cardiovascular Research Volume 54, Issue2 Pp. 217-229.

Santoli, S. (2003). *"Is there an Advanced Placement Advantage?"* American Secondary Education, 30(3), Summer.

www.enchantedlearning.com/subjects/anatomy/heart/labelin terior/label.shtml

THE LAST WORD

The Target Construction and Rubric Construction templates in this publication were meant as a temporary guide. Once a teacher becomes a fluid target and rubric creator, these templates will no longer be needed.

The other teacher templates are meant for continual use to identify student progress toward meeting skill and content based standards. The teacher can then diagnose and repair gaps in learning.

This publication is the product of years of teaching and a belief that teachers are educational experts. Teachers should be encouraged to publish. They should be encouraged by their districts, principals and most importantly by other teachers.

Once teachers become comfortable publishing their work, pedagogy will ultimately change. When teachers are seen as experts, education will take a much needed turn towards true reform.

TEMPLATE APPENDIX

Target Construction Template

State Standard:

If the state standard has more than one component, list each below with the supporting content.
•
•
•
Select one of the above components for target construction.

Determine the complexity according to Bloom's. List complexity level below.
Complexity Level_____
Alternate words that can be used for component verb:

I can _____   _____
action component verb   *use student friendly language for content*

Target Check List
Make sure your target has:
o   No numbers
o   Single sentence
o   A single verb
o   Age appropriate vocabulary
o   Important to the content
o   No language that is outside of target content *(i.e. complete in ink, neatness)*

Other learning associated with this standard:

Rubric Construction Template

Topic:

Unit:

State Standard Classification:

State Standard:

Target:

Rubric Title:

Incomplete Evidence of Learning (I)	Level 1: Foundation for Target	Level 2: Progressing Toward Target Proficiency	Level 3: Target Proficiency	Level 4: Advanced Application of Target
	I can…	I can…	I can…	I can…

D. Elder © 2012   97

General Unit Map Template

General Unit Map				
Content Area:				
State Standard:				
Learning Target (s):				
Rubric Title:				

Incomplete Evidence of Learning (I)	Level 1 Foundational for Target	Level 2 Progressing Toward Target Proficiency	Level 3 Target Proficiency	Level 4 Advanced Application of Target
	(lower level Bloom's) I can …	(middle level Bloom's) I can…	(upper level Bloom's) I can…	(high Bloom's) I can…

Unit Detail Section		
Date Days	**Elicitation Question:**	**Main idea:**
	Unit Introduction:	
	Level 1 Activities:	
	Level 2 Activities:	

	Level 3 Activities:	
	Study Guide for all levels:	
	Level 1, 2, 3 Assessment:	
	Re-teach Session:	
Teacher Resources:		

Unit Planning Guide Template

Unit Planning Guide
Content Area:
State Standard:
Learning Target (s): **Rubric Title:**

Incomplete Evidence of Learning (I)	Level 1 Foundational for Target	Level 2 Progressing Toward Target Proficiency	Level 3 Target Proficiency	Level 4 Advanced Application of Target
	(lower level Bloom's) I can …	(middle level Bloom's) I can…	(upper level Bloom's) I can…	(high Bloom's) I can…

5-E Learning Cycle: **E1:** Engage   **E2:** Explore   **E3:** Explain   **E4:** Extend   **E5:** Evaluate

Date	5-E Learning Cycle	Rubric Level	Content:	Activities:	Class period

Table of Contents

Date	Level	Assignment Name	Page #	Score

Multitarget Journal Rubric Template

Level	1	2	3

Target(s) that will be assessed are:

Student Reflection:
My assessment of my journal is **level**…
Because:

Teacher Reflection:
Assessment of this student journal is **level**…
Because:

My plan to improve or maintain journal is:

Study Guide Template

Study Guide Name:

Level 1: *(general description)*

Define and draw the following:

	Define:	Draw:
 • • • •		

Level 2: *(general description)*

Level 3: *(general description)*

- ○ I can complete level 1 without assistance

- ○ I can complete level 1 without assistance

- ○ I can complete level 3 without assistance

If I can not complete each level without assistance, I plan to (circle one): Ask the teacher for help, ask a friend for help, review work from my journal or_____.

Effort and Achievement Reflection Rubric Template

	Effort Reflection		Achievement Reflection
3	I worked to understand what was taught by asking questions when stuck, completing assignments in class, studying for the assessment	3	Using my study guide to assess what I learned, I can prove I can understand level 3
2	I worked to complete work and understand what was taught but I did not always stay focused, review work or ask questions	2	Using my study guide to assess what I learned, I can prove I can understand level 2
1	I put some effort into my journal but I did not understand what was taught	1	Using my study guide to assess what I learned, I can prove I can understand level 1
I	I have not put effort into my learning	I	I did not understand the study guide

(I= Incomplete effort or achievement)

Assessment Name:
Assessment Score:

Post Assessment Reflection:
I can explain:
- Assessment score and **effort** reflection:

- Assessment score and **achievement** reflection:

Goal Setting
- **Effort Goal** for next assessment:

- How I will reach my effort goal:

- **Achievement Goal** for next assessment:

- How I will reach my achievement goal:

Level 1 Reteach Template

Vocabulary Terms	Definition	Quiz another (check off when done)	You are quizzed (check off when done)

Trial assessment:

Vocabulary Terms	Definition for each:

Ready to take the assessment?

Reteach for Level 2 and 3 Template

Before Reteach Session	After Reteach Session
<ul><li>I shared my improvement with my partner.</li><li>My partner explained her/his improvements to me.</li><li>I explained my improvements to the teacher.</li></ul>	

About the Author

Danelle Elder has three degrees from Eastern Washington University: B.A. of Education; B.S. in Geology and a M.S. Interdisciplinary degree, (Geology and Education).

She was a geologist before she was teacher. She has taught for over 25 years as a middle school science teacher. She has taught at Whitworth University in the state of Washington.

She was born in Richland, Washington, but lives in Spokane Washington.

Contact and consulting information:
Email: daniellelder5702@comcast.net
Website: http://standardbasedteaching.com

Made in the USA
San Bernardino, CA
19 April 2014

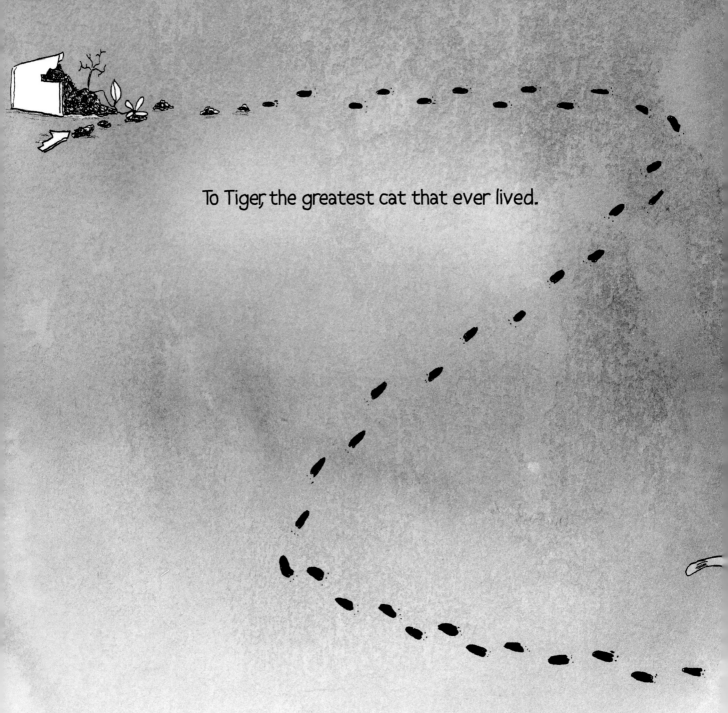

To Tiger, the greatest cat that ever lived.

ISBN 9781976582301
First Bookshelf Edition, November 2017.
www.yvonnepage.com

Stinky Poo

Written & Illustrated by
Yvonne Page

To Uncle Ken + Aunt Diana,
To read to the
Puppies :)

Yvonne Page
4/18

J.J.R. Press

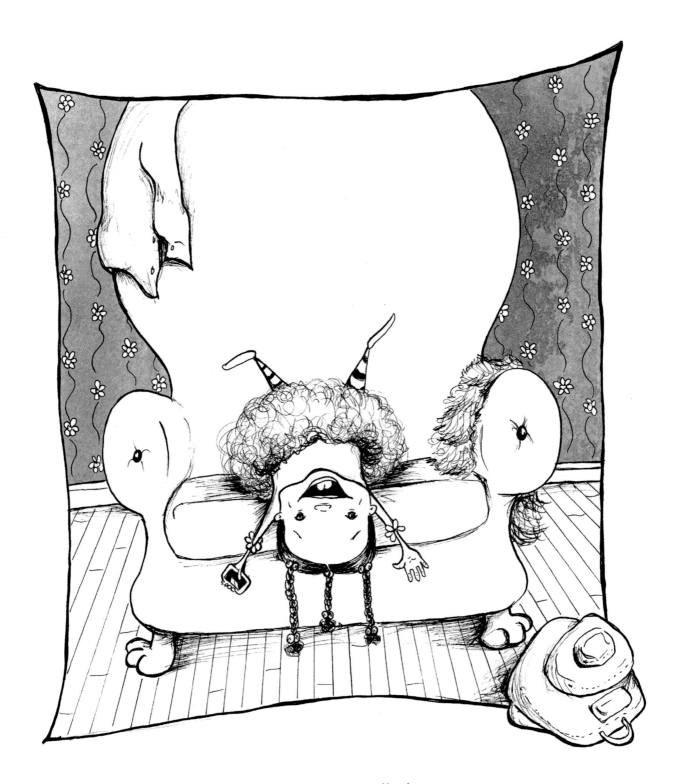

When her mother called to say
she was bringing home a surprise,
Victoria knew exactly what it would be.

She was sure that
absolutely,
positively,
without a doubt,
her surprise would be...

a puppy.

It was not a puppy.
Not at all.

Not even a little.

Victoria's surprise was a

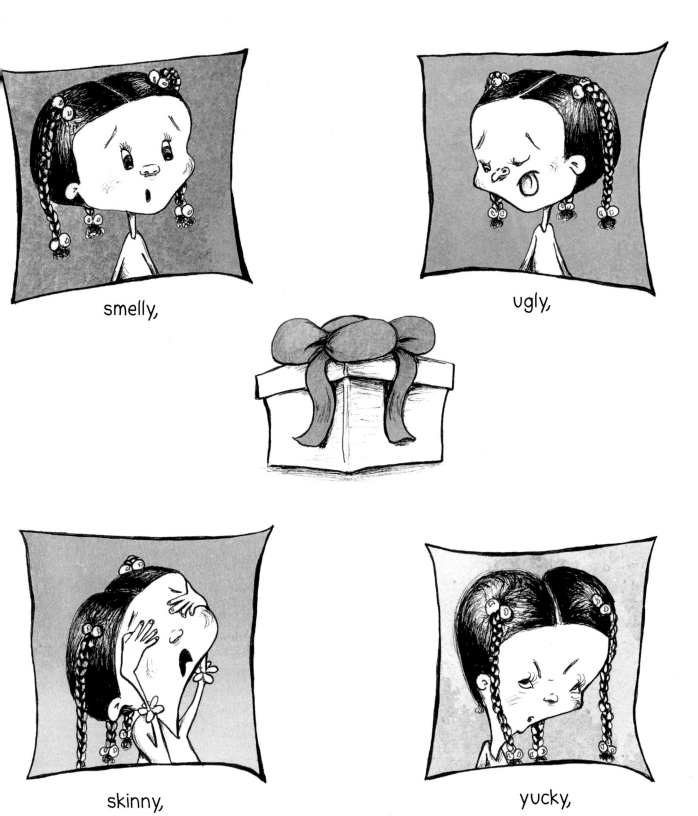

smelly,

ugly,

skinny,

yucky,

CAT!

Victoria was horrified.

In fact, this cat was so yucky and so smelly that
Victoria decided to name him "Stinky Poo."

"Maybe a bath will help," said her mom.

Maybe.

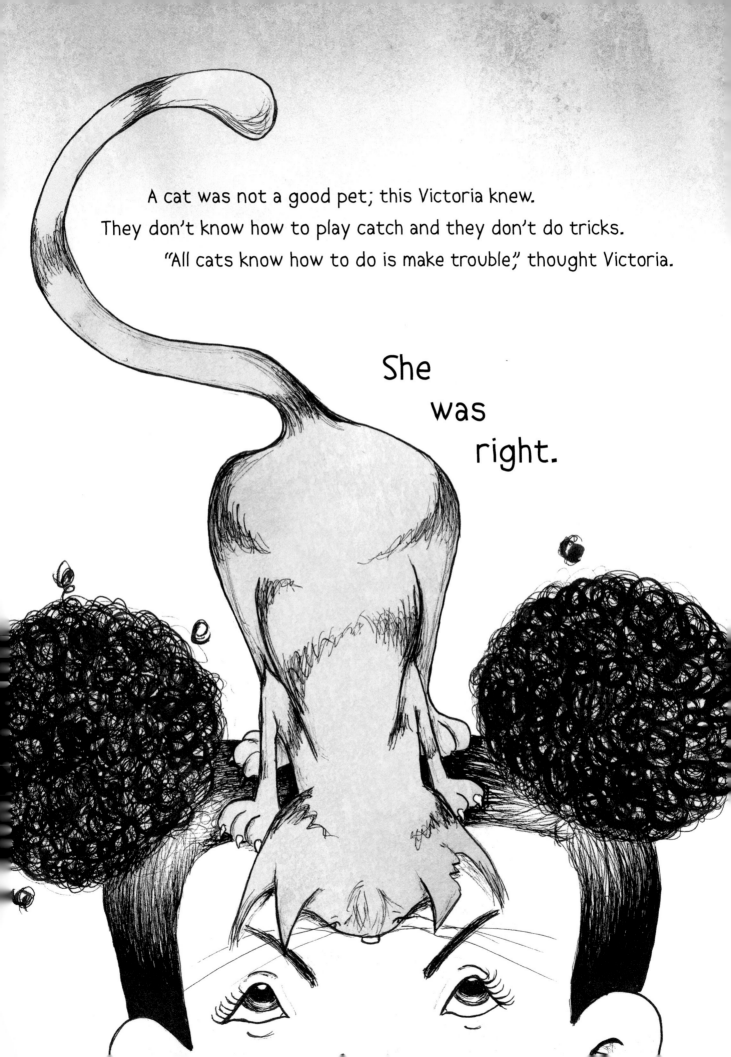

A cat was not a good pet; this Victoria knew.
They don't know how to play catch and they don't do tricks.
"All cats know how to do is make trouble," thought Victoria.

She
was
right.

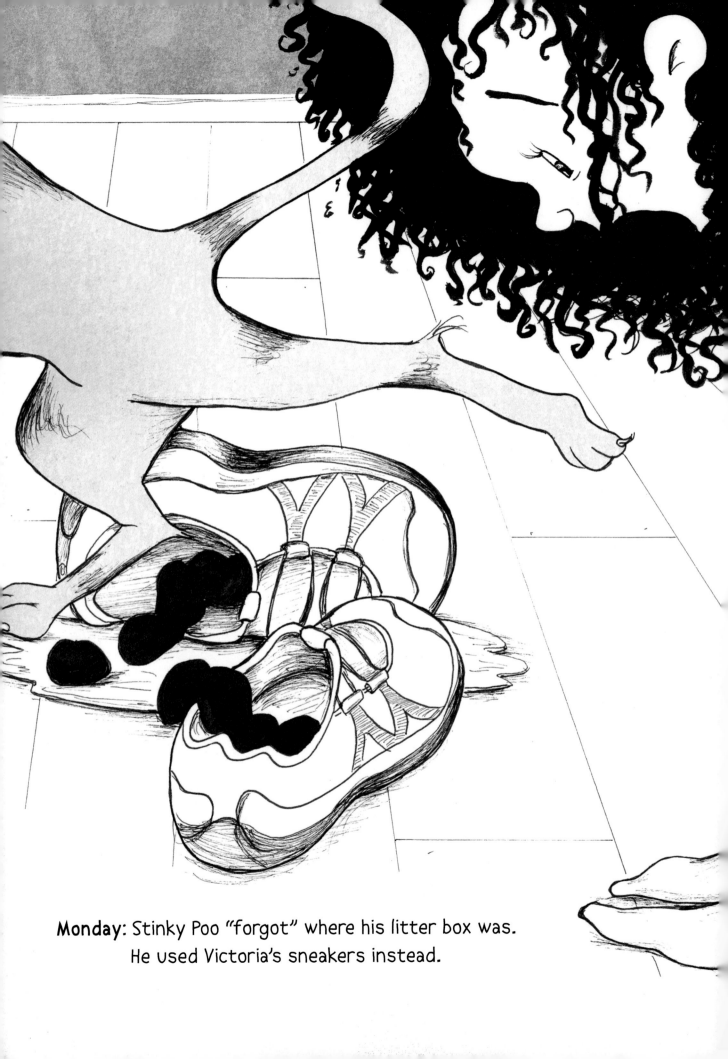

Monday: Stinky Poo "forgot" where his litter box was.
He used Victoria's sneakers instead.

Tuesday: *That cat* ate
Victoria's tuna fish sandwich out of her
lunch box while she was getting ready for school.

She had to eat peanut butter and jelly.

Wednesday: Stinky Poo took a nap
in Victoria's favorite chair.

She had to sit in the broken chair.

Thursday: He erased Victoria's whole book report.

Friday: Stinky Poo ate her favorite doll.

By the end of the week, Victoria was just plain fed up!

So, Stinky Poo went away.

Far, far away.
Never to return.

And Victoria was all alone.

She had no one
to play with

and no one to
dance with.

She had no one to
give her gifts

and no one to fight
monsters with.

Victoria was sad.
She missed Stinky Poo.

But by now, he was nowhere to be found.

"Oh Stinky Poo, where are you? Please come back," she cried.
"You're my best friend!"

And so, Stinky Poo came back
and he kissed her and he hugged her,

and he let her dress him up like a baby.

So, Victoria decided that Stinky Poo was
the best pet in the whole world.

Even better than a puppy.

(Turn the page for more fun!)

Coloring & Activity Section

Bet you didn't know you could write or color in a picture book, did you? Well, in this one you can! The next few pages are filled with activities and pages that YOU can color. When you're finished, take a picture of your artwork and stories and upload them to yvonnepage.com to share your work with the world! On the website you'll also find even more fun coloring pages and activities that are free for you to download and use!

Help Stinky Poo Get Back Home to Victoria!

Stinky Poo's Favorite Things Word Find

Can you find these 10 things that Stinky Poo loves so much?
They are up, down, or diagonal!

Tuna	Home	Naps	Chewing	Boxes
Victoria	Toys	Scratching	Catnip	String

```
A D S L E T H I B K O M
C B C N A P S P O T L U
H A C D T M P I X N O V
E B T D G U Y L E K R I
W I C N E P H I S H L C
I R C D I G V O J O L T
N B C Q E P Y I M K N O
G X T U N A H I J E L R
B A O Y D G R N O K L I
R P Y D E Z H I J K L A
Y T S C R A T C H I N G
A S T R I N G N J K T M
```

Write Your Own Story!

Fill in the blanks to tell your own story about Stinky Poo and Victoria!

It was a cold, rainy day. Victoria and Stinky Poo were bored.

"I know what we can do", exclaimed Victoria. "We can
_____ in the _____!"

They were having a _____ time _____
when they heard a noise. When they went to check, they
saw that it was _____ . Stinky Poo was
_____ . Victoria _____ .
They decided to _____ .

After that, they thought it might be best to
_____ with a _____ .

Finally, it was time for dinner. They ate _____
and it tasted _____ . Stinky Poo ate _____ bowls!
After dinner, they _____ and then went to bed.

The End!

Yvonne Page is a freelance writer and illustrator. Her work has been featured in many magazines and publications and she is the illustrator of the *Super Cool Scientists* coloring book. *Stinky Poo* is Yvonne's first picture book and was inspired by her lifelong love of cats.

When she's not drawing or painting, Yvonne's favorite thing to do is spend time with her family, their two dogs, and cat.

Get Even More on the Website

Visit yvonnepage.com for free coloring pages and activities, to listen to this book read by the author, and for other cool stuff!